When Love Bends Down

When Love Bends Down

IMAGES OF THE CHRIST WHO
MEETS US WHERE WE ARE

BY
MICHAEL LODAHL

BEACON HILL PRESS
OF KANSAS CITY

Library of Congress Cataloging-in-Publication Data

Lodahl, Michael E., 1955-
   When love bends down : images of the Christ who meets us where we are /
by Michael Lodahl.
      p. cm.
   ISBN-13: 978-0-8341-2220-8 (pbk.)
   ISBN-10: 0-8341-2220-0 (pbk.)
   1. Jesus Christ—Person and offices. 2. God—Love. 3. God—Mercy. 4.
Love—Religious aspects—Christianity. I. Title.

   BT203.L64 2006
   232.9'03—dc22

                                                      2006014603

10 9 8 7 6 5 4 3 2 1

For C. S. Cowles and Reuben Welch:
a pair of inspiring teachers of a
Christ-shaped theology, their lives faithfully
embody what their lips profess.

CONTENTS

INTRODUCTION

The earliest inspiration for this little book was another book, titled *No Handle on the Cross,* by Japanese theologian Kosuke Koyama. It is a wonderful book, a model of practical Christian theology at its readable best.[1]

In one of his chapters, Koyama offers a theological meditation on the story of the woman who, having been caught in adultery, was dragged out into the light of Jerusalem's most public square, the Temple, to face Jesus (John 8:1-11). Koyama mindfully notes the Gospel description of Jesus' dramatic physical response to the humiliating situation: "Jesus bent down and wrote with his finger on the ground" (v. 6). Since in chapter 1 that soon follows I will draw heavily on Koyama's moving interpretation of this story, suffice it to say that the portrait of Jesus *bent down* provides for us a marvelous image for thinking about Jesus—and thus also for thinking about God.

That story, however, is the only one that Koyama reads with the help of this concept of the bent-down Jesus. In the years that followed my reading of his book, though, it began to occur to me that this story was not alone in John's Gospel. Far from it! I saw that in fact the Gospel of John seems to have a distinct preference for stories of Jesus that portray Him in a bent-down way. For several years now, those stories

have provided the gist for a collection of sermons cele-
brating the bent-down Jesus.

But as those sermons took shape over time, it became increasingly clear to me that it wasn't enough to
talk about a bent-down Jesus. A bent-down Jesus must
imply something about the way His followers live as the
Church together. I have since my teenage years loved
the New Testament Epistle called 1 John—especially
since the time in my late teens when I read *We Really
Do Need Each Other* by Reuben Welch, religion professor emeritus at Point Loma Nazarene University. It
eventually dawned on me that I might try to connect
the bent-down stories of Jesus in John's Gospel with
complementary passages regarding the Church in John's
first letter. That is what I have tried to do, with God's
help, in this little book.

I could not have dreamed back when I read Professor Welch's book on 1 John that the time would
come when this wonderful man of the Bible would be
my Sunday School teacher and friend, or for that matter that I would be a theology professor at Point Loma
myself. Since I could not and did not dream either of
those things, they are not dreams come true—they are
much better! It is an unspeakably rich blessing in my
life to be able to learn with fellow classmates in Reuben's Sojourners class; obviously our year-or-so sojourn
through the Gospel of John a while back was especially
helpful to me in polishing these little meditations. It is
equally a joy to teach theology in such a beautiful set-

ting, with such inspiring and encouraging colleagues as we have at Point Loma. It was in a series of four university chapel services in the fall of 2000 that I first was given the opportunity to preach the bent-down stories of John's Gospel as a continuous theme. When the series was over, Dr. Patrick Allen, our faculty provost, encouraged me to "write a little book on bent-down theology." I try to do what my boss tells me.

More recently, I was privileged and humbled to fill the role of revival speaker for Olivet Nazarene University and College Church of the Nazarene in Kankakee, Illinois, during the fall of 2004. The warm Christian hospitality of Olivet chaplain Michael Benson and President John Bowling, and the eager receptivity of the students and faculty in the chapel services, were great gifts of joy and encouragement. Likewise, right across the street, Pastors Dan Boone and Jeff Crosno were, as always, models of the bent-down Jesus I came to their church to proclaim. With pastors such as they, it is no wonder that the College Church congregation exudes the welcoming, warm love of the Body of Christ. In that rewarding setting for preaching the gospel, I was able to sharpen the connections between the bent-down stories of Jesus in the Gospel of John and the passages from 1 John to be explored in this book.

During that same fall, Point Loma granted me a sabbatical to work on several writing projects, of which this book is one. I am deeply grateful for that time to read, reflect, travel, and write. I especially want to give thanks for Point Loma's Wesleyan Center for Twenty-First Century Studies. There, the help and hospitality of Robin Evans and Sharon Bowles made coming to the campus a pleasure, even on sabbatical.

There was one other gathering of sisters and brothers with whom I shared the recurring Johannine theme of the bent-down Jesus. It was for the Pastors and Spouses' Retreat for the Church of the Nazarene, Anaheim District, in the fall of 2003. Before our retreat time was finished, one of the ministers there, Elena Gonzalez, translated this theme into poetry and music. Accompanied by guitar, Elena ministered to us all by singing her composition. While it is, of course, not the same as hearing this beautiful song, with her permission I share her lyrics with you as a fitting conclusion to this introduction.

He Bent Down
Elena Gonzalez

Our Christ bent down, wrote on the ground,
And all the while the crowd milled around.
There she stood with eyes of shame,
Waiting to hear what Christ would say.
He stood and said, "The law is clear;
What she has done will cost life dear.
So if you please, if you are sure,
Let him cast stone whose heart is pure."

Refrain:
Yes, Jesus bent to do His work,

Down to the ground, down in the dirt.
He came from heav'n to earth below,
Humbled himself, His love to show.

Our Christ bent down, spit on the ground.
A man stood still, dark eyes cast down.
His whole life in the darkness lay
Until the Healer came his way.
"Go wash the mud from eyes unclear,
Go wash the dirt in pool so near."
And when the man washed mud away
Sight was restored that very day.

Our Christ bent down with towel in hand,
With basin full to wash the sand
From His friends' feet, sitting in that room.
He knew His time was coming soon.
He washed their feet and toweled them dry,
He did each one without a sigh.
"You must do this for those you lead,
A humble heart will grow love's seed."

Our Christ bent down to tend the flame,
Just as before; He seemed the same.
And on that boat they realized
It was the Christ, the Crucified.
He waited there upon that shore,
Tended their needs, their hearts were sore.
"If you love Me, then tend My sheep,
In My love help them to grow deep."

John 8:6

JESUS BENT DOWN AND WROTE WITH
HIS FINGER ON THE GROUND.

The Bent-Down Theology of Jesus

I remember that Sunday morning so very well. I was freshly graduated from seminary, a brand-new pastor still wet behind the ears, as green as they come. On that Sunday morning I trudged to the pulpit with butterflies in the pit of my stomach. My knees felt like jelly as I looked out into the expectant faces of the congregation. I opened my notebook and discovered I had forgotten my sermon notes. But much worse, I discovered that I'd also forgotten my pants.

Happily, I then woke up. Several hours later on that Sunday morning I walked up to that pulpit again—for real, this time—armed with my notes and legged with my pants. I'd made sure on both counts.

I was to learn later that such dreams are common among preachers and other public figures, and in fact I have had more of those dreams myself. But the commonality of the experience has not dissipated the feelings of embarrassment that, though it was but a dream, were still very real that early Sunday morn in bed.

Those feelings, however, are nothing compared to the situation of the woman described in John 8:1-11. This was a woman caught dead in the act of adultery by what can accurately be called a gang of men; this was a woman forced out of bed and out of the house, likely with nothing more than a blanket draped around her body; this was a woman dragged into the presence of Jesus and His disciples, thoroughly shamed and humiliated. She may have wished it was just a dream—in this case, a nightmare—but there was no simple waking up from this terrifying scene.

It is hard to imagine a more humiliating situation —or a more frightening situation! For we can readily assume that this woman, presumably a Jew, knew the Torah well enough to know that it was plain as day on this matter: "If a man is found sleeping with another man's wife, both the man who slept with her and the woman must die. You must purge the evil from Israel" (Deut. 22:22, NIV)—and such purging was to occur by stoning both of them to death. The prospects did not look good for this vulnerable, humiliated, embarrassed, and threatened woman.

One of the things, though, that we should ponder before proceeding any further is that only the woman was brought before Jesus. Where's the guy? Both were condemned to death by the Law of Moses, but there's no man in this picture. Why not? After all, it takes two for adultery to happen. Why was this woman singled out?

A point to consider is that in any society where women are treated essentially as sexual objects—which, by the way, is of course precisely what pornography is—it is not unusual to consider the woman to be the guilty party, the dirty temptress, and to dismiss the man as somehow innocent in the matter. In that light, it is significant that this group of so-called righteous men, self-proclaimed defenders of God's holy Law, conveniently overlooked the adulterous man in their little lynching party. I suppose it is possible that he escaped; the text does not say. But perhaps we should also wonder how this woman had been caught in the act at all; is it not possible that her partner had actually been a part of the trap? In that case, this woman was being hung out to dry by someone she thought had feelings for her. So, no matter how we decide to fill in the blanks of this passage, what is certain is that this woman is feeling totally abandoned at this moment. She is surrounded by righteous rage and sanctimonious hatred—and is utterly alone.

The text tells us that it really wasn't even the woman that these champions of morality were after. She was only the bait with which to snag Jesus. And I suspect they felt they had Jesus pretty well cornered. On the one hand, the laws of Moses were clear on this point: Adulterers must be stoned till they are dead. On the other hand, there is a reliable historical tradition that informs us that, by this time, the Roman occupying government had prohibited the Jewish legal body, the Sanhedrin, from carrying out the Torah's death penalties. Perhaps, as in other instances, the idea was that they would get Jesus in trouble with one of two factions. On the one hand, the most conservative Jews would see Jesus as being lax in the matter of enforcing Moses' laws—that He was soft on adultery—and would therefore accuse Him of overturning the very commands of God. On the other hand, if Jesus took the literalist path regarding Deuteronomy, He could get into hot water with the Romans by prescribing capital punishment. In a sense, these religious leaders had drawn a line in the sand and dared Jesus to step over it—or not—and possibly to face serious trouble either way.

In the construction of their little trap, they were quite willing to humiliate, denigrate, and dehumanize this woman in order to accomplish their goals. The point is not to minimize her adultery but to remember nonetheless that she was a human being, a woman who, while nameless to us, had a name. Can you imagine how she felt as she cowered there in the city street, trying to cover herself, her shame being exposed in Jerusalem's public spaces? This is about as ugly as the human spirit can get, and one gets the feeling that the entire escapade simply made Jesus sick.

One of my favorite theologians, Japanese missionary-scholar Kosuke Koyama, has offered a compelling interpretation of this story that provides the inspiration for this meditation and indeed for this entire book. In his book *No Handle on the Cross*, Koyama calls this story of the woman caught in adultery a "bent down" story. As this humiliated woman was thrown at Jesus' feet and made into bait to entrap Him, *Jesus bent down and wrote with his finger on the ground.*

What an odd thing to do! What did Jesus write? Of course, nobody knows. Isn't it interesting that Jesus didn't write down anything that we know of? No essays penned by our Teacher, no books authored. And this one time when we are told that He wrote something, we are *not* told what it was! Apparently Jesus didn't get caught up in getting His teachings all down on papyrus just right; instead, He was content to teach, to make His disciples, to live His teaching with them, and to entrust those teachings and that kind of living to them. Some of us Christian believers have a real obsession about the written word—it's just interesting that Jesus didn't. In this very Gospel, in fact, Jesus said to some of the great Jewish scribes, experts in the written Word, "You search the scriptures because you think that in them you have eternal life" (John 5:39a). And that is the way some (indeed, many) people look at the Bible even today, as though it is itself the source of eternal life. But the Bible is not an end in itself. For Jesus continued, "And it is they [these scriptures] that testify on my behalf" (v. 39b). In other words, the

Scriptures exercise the function of pointing us *toward Jesus* as the One in whom there is divine life, love, and grace. The Scriptures point us toward Him, toward hearing Him and obeying His Word, toward a daily walk with the living Christ.

It is likely no coincidence that this Gospel is the one that begins by identifying the Word not as something that is first of all *written,* but as something that is first of all *living, creative,* and indeed *divine.* "In the beginning was the Word, and the Word was with God, and the Word was God" (1:1). It is this very Word that "became flesh and lived among us" (v. 14), and that incarnate Word is none other than Jesus. *Jesus is the Word, God's very Word, spoken into becoming a human life, a human being, in this world.* In a similar vein, the letter to the Hebrews opens by declaring that God "has spoken to us by [His] Son" (v. 2)—underscoring for us this Christian conviction that Jesus himself is God's ultimate communication, God's very Word, to the world. When God speaks, God's language is *Jesus.*

Ignatius, the early second-century martyr and bishop of Antioch, lived and died for this same truth. When Jewish critics questioned whether the gospel he preached was supported by "the original documents" (the Hebrew Scriptures), Ignatius retorted: "To my mind it is Jesus Christ who is the original documents. The inviolable archives are his cross and death and his resurrection and the faith that came by him."[2] We should see, then, that the written Word of the Bible has as its purpose to testify to God's Living Word, Jesus himself. Jesus apparently did not make a habit of writing down words; rather, His very life is Divine Word. And in the passage before us, when He finally does bend down to write, it is in the dirt! Not only are we not told what He wrote, but it is obvious that writing in the sand is a great way to guarantee that one's words will be forgotten. Words scrawled in the dirt are bound to be effaced, walked upon, scruffed and scuffled over. No written words here—we are left instead with the image of Jesus, bent down, scrawling in the sand.

We can press this point further. Even a cursory glance at the notes in most Bibles will inform us that this written passage itself (John 7:53—8:11) is not a part of the earliest manuscripts of John's Gospel available to us. Those same notes may inform you that this story can also be found at the end of John in some of our oldest manuscripts. For that matter, there are a few manuscripts that even have this story in a different Gospel altogether!—it is found in some, but not many, manuscripts of the Gospel of Luke (after 21:38). What do these multiple locations for this story suggest? I take this manuscript evidence to imply that this was a very popular story of Jesus' ministry that circulated throughout many of the early churches, probably as an oral tradition. Once it was written down, apparently it floated around looking for a textual place to call home. So, though it was not part of any of our earliest written Gospels, the Church refused to let this "dangerous memory" of Jesus fade into oblivion. The words Jesus scrawled in the dirt may have become lost to us, but not the story itself. One can only assume that second-century Christians kept telling this story, kept looking for a place to put it in their written testimonies about Jesus, precisely because it was so thoroughly true to Jesus' spirit and ministry. It was a testimony to Jesus that refused to die.

Thus, we are confronted by a story of Jesus that is all the more powerful, all the more compelling, for its rather tenuous place in written testimony. For indeed, in this very story Jesus raises a prophetic critique against overly literalistic and harsh interpretations of the written Word. What is written is not the final or ultimate arbiter; had it been, Jesus would have had to join the mob of stone-toting men who surrounded the adulterer. Further, in this very story Jesus the Living Word bends down to the dirt and writes—what? Even Jesus' own written word is not deemed of sufficient importance to be shared with us who read the story. And of course, whatever Jesus did write was trampled and lost within the hour. This word written in the dirt is effaced, erased, disappearing in shifting sands—but the Living Word remains.

Indeed, it is entirely possible that Jesus did not write anything at all. The Greek word in this text can just as readily mean that Jesus doodled or scribbled in the sand. I tend to prefer this possibility—that perhaps Jesus was embarrassed for this woman, so He cast His eyes and attention downward to the ground. Perhaps His blood was boiling at these men who had done this, and He is trying to cool down—just kind of scribbling down there for a minute, counting to 10 slowly. Who can know for certain? No matter how we interpret this bent-down moment, Koyama's insights are probing:

> This is another "bent down" story. The story does far more than criticize the legalism of the scribes and Pharisees. Jesus did not reject Moses. He deepened Moses. . . . In this act of deepening, the position of Jesus was clear and simple; . . . Indeed [said Jesus] Moses was right! Let us follow his law. *But* let us not follow it with a crusading mind . . . but in the crucified mind. . . .
>
> "Jesus bent down and wrote with his finger on the ground" as if he was calling the earth, the whole created world, to witness this event of deepening. . . . While he "bent down" (a "foolish and weak" posture!), he prepared his deepening of the spiritual tradition of Moses and Israel.[3]

There is something about Jesus bent down here that thoroughly captivates our minds and hearts. Jesus, low to the ground; Jesus, finger moving slowly through the sand; Jesus, dropping so low as to be on the same level as this frightened and humiliated woman, sprawled in the sand. I love this Jesus who *could*, who *can*, and who *does bend down* to where I am, *down* to where you are—and who loves you and me with a love that will not let us go.

As Jesus bent down and scrawled into the very earth itself, Koyama argues, He was at the same time digging into the heart and deepest intent of the Torah, the Law of Moses. "[Go ahead and stone her,]" He said, "but let anyone among you who is without sin be the first to throw" (v. 7). Jesus' finger was now scrawling into hardened human hearts. One by one, these zealous defenders of literalism who had turned the Torah into a rock for beating people dropped their clenched fists, stones slipping to the ground, and slipped away.

Koyama is right; Jesus did not try to escape the situation, nor did He gloss over its inhumane injustice. He deepened the situation, His finger probing the secrets within us just as surely as the ground beneath us. He pushed through to the other side of the Torah, into the very heart of the God of mercy.

I cannot escape an image from my youth. It is a powerful visual memory of a man bent down to the ground, finger digging, probing in the dirt. The man, in this case, was a firefighter.

As a boy I loved, absolutely loved, to play with matches. I loved to create flames, loved to burn little plastic soldiers and ants and other little-boy targets. One lazy Sunday afternoon, while my parents napped, I took a book of matches out into the backyard and began to construct an imaginative scenario. I was a super-spy, saving the world from the biggest payload of dynamite ever amassed. How'd I do it? The bad guys had lit the fuse—which happened to be a piece of string tied to a ladder that was leaning against our house. I had to beat all of those invisible, imaginary bad guys—at least six or seven of them—in hand-to-hand combat before I could reach the fuse and blow it out. But I did it! The big explosion was averted! I snuffed the flame! The fuse was extinguished! All was safe with the world . . . I thought.

To celebrate my heroic victory I went next door to the Thomas family backyard and climbed up into their old tire swing, hanging from a big weeping willow. Ah, lazy Sunday afternoons are wonderful for world-saving young heroes! I don't know how long I swung back and forth, and around in circles, in that tire. But it was long enough that by the time I swaggered back to my backyard, flames were consuming our house.

I rushed in, crying out, "The house is on fire!"

"Call the fire department!" my mom, roused from her Sunday nap, yelled back. Of course I dutifully did just that, and it was not long before the big red truck rumbled up the alleyway, into our backyard, and the real heroes quickly put out the fire. I hoped—but did not pray—that everyone would simply be happy that the fire was contained and the house saved. I hoped—but did not pray—that everyone would simply assume that faulty wiring in the walls was to blame. One can always hope.

But then there's that inescapable image—a fireman bent down to the wet, ashy ground, digging around with his finger. That man was bent down to the ground, not content simply to put out the fire. That man was probing, poking, seeking some deeper reason for the fire. I did not want that man to be probing. I wanted us all just to offer our applause and thanks to the Othello, Washington, Fire Department and let it go at that.

But like Jesus in our story, this man was not content to live with an easy answer. He was probing; he was deepening the situation. And in that blackened mud, he found what he was digging for—matches.

I am not proud of what I did next. With most of the neighborhood gathered around the muddy, smoking scene, I looked around at all those familiar faces and quickly noted that Heidi Chambers, the tomboy who lived directly across the alley from us, was not part of the crowd. Now the 10-year-old superspy turned into an amateur detective: "Hmm," I observed suspiciously, "I just wonder where *Heidi Chambers is right now!* Why isn't *she* here?"

Never mind that Heidi was gone for the entire day, visiting her grandma with the rest of her family. I didn't know it at the time and was only interested in shifting the blame elsewhere. I would have been happy to blame it on Heidi's grandma if I could. It was a uniquely human talent I was developing, not at all unlike the kind of phony righteousness of the accusers in our Gospel story. But with both the fireman and with Jesus, we find someone who is probing the earth, and probing us, and trying to dig down to the real issues. I

might have at least temporarily dodged the probing
finger of that fireman, but the woman's accusers were
dealing with someone whose finger can dig much deeper: This is the finger of the Word who became flesh—
flesh and bone and body and blood—and lived among
us as the God-Man. Their guilt exposed, they slipped
away in shame.

Notice verse 10: "Jesus straightened up and said
to her, 'Woman, where are they?' Has no one condemned you?'" It could just as easily be translated that
Jesus "looked up" and asked her these rhetorical questions; hence, Koyama writes:

> Jesus is speaking to her from the lower posi-
> tion, the position of being "bent down." "Woman,
> where are they . . . ?' She said, "No one, Lord."
> Jesus took her word. . . . On the basis of her ob-
> servation (!) Jesus said simply: "Neither do I con-
> demn you; go, and do not sin again." He over-
> looked all "important theological questions"! Why
> did he say "neither do I condemn you"? He did
> not give any reason for doing this. He deepened
> the situation and in his deepening he exercised his
> freedom. "Neither do I condemn you" derives
> from "bent-down theology."[4]

What a powerful conversation! In this crucial moment of encounter with the Christ who can bend down
and scrawl in the sand, Koyama suggests that the "cru-
sading mind of the scribes and Pharisees experienced
crucifixion" of sorts, while the woman experienced a

resurrection into the grace and new possibilities of
God. "By deepening it," Koyama writes, "Jesus healed
the ugly situation. What a spiritual power had this man
who 'bent down'! By deepening"[5]—by being willing to
get down on ground level, to probe the hearts of those
who had the Bible on their side, rather than by manip-
ulating or coercing or bullying or throwing His weight
around—Jesus brought healing. "Indeed, God did not
send the Son into the world to condemn the world, but
in order that the world might be saved through him"
(John 3:17).

What humble, gentle grace this is—and thus also a
grace that can make this demand, "Go and sin no more"
(NKJV). (It was the kind of grace my own parents demonstrated toward their pyromaniac boy, thanks be to
God.) What a Savior is this who bends down—down low
to where we are in this very moment. Where others
condemn and throw stones, Jesus bends down. Jesus
probes the situation, unafraid to dig deep into the situation of our lives and to call us forth into new life.
Hear the words He says to you: "Neither do I condemn
you; go and sin no more" (8:11, NKJV). These words are
offered to us all by the One who is *bent down*.

John 9:25

ONE THING I DO KNOW. I WAS BLIND
BUT NOW I SEE! *(NIV)*.

A Bent-Down Healing of Jesus

The testimony of a man blind from birth, whose story is told in John 9, has etched its way deeply into Christian hymnody:

I once was lost, but now am found;
was blind, but now I see.

It is no surprise that his experience has provided language for our own, for this man's plain account of what happened to him when he met Jesus has an undeniable power. While the Pharisees who questioned him wanted to debate the finer points of Jewish theology, this unnamed man stuck very close to his story: "He put mud on my eyes, . . . and I washed, and now I see. . . . Whether he is a sinner or not, I don't know. One thing I do know. I was blind but now I see!" (vv. 15, 25, NIV).

We know that there are many accounts in our Gospels of the wondrous healings and miracles of Jesus; here in John's Gospel, they are typically called "signs." But for all of those mighty works, as far as I can recall I have never heard a sermon or lecture that addresses this portrait of Jesus in John 9: Jesus spitting into the dust, molding a homemade mudpack, and plastering it to the eyes of a blind man. That's just not the kind of stuff that preaching and theology are usually made of—dirt and spit and mud and the like. As we ponder this picture of Jesus bent low to the ground, rolling a pair of little mud plasters between His fingers, I invite you not only to think with me about the wondrous grace of God in Christ to restore this man's sight but also to reflect with me about *how* Jesus went about doing it.

Since we are on the subject, let us consider that this is not the only time in the Gospels that we read of Jesus using spit. There are two other such instances, both in the Book of Mark: in one case Jesus spits on His fingers and touches the tongue of a man who could not talk, and in the words of Mark, "his tongue was loosed, and he spoke plainly" (Mark 7:35, NKJV). In the other case, Jesus just spat into the eyes of a blind man and then put His hands on the man's eyes, and in what Mark describes as a kind of gradual process—a two-step healing—Jesus restored his sight.

The notable difference of these two stories in Mark from the passage before us in John is that in this case, we encounter another *bent-down* story. On the strength of this passage and the others we will exam-

ine, I submit to you that John likes bent-down stories
—I *think* he thinks that they tell us something about
Jesus' character and ministry, and thus also that they
tell us something about *God.* Just as we explored the
image of Jesus bending down to write or scrawl or doo-
dle in the sand before the humiliated woman caught in
the act of adultery and forcibly dragged into the public
presence of Jesus, so now we find Jesus again *bending
down,* getting down there to work the dirt a little. Jesus does not stand high over the man and simply command his eyes to open up; He gets down, probably
down on His knees, and works up a *healing salve* for
this poor man who had never seen a sunset, who had
never looked into another person's eyes, who had never
beheld the beauty of a woman or the wonder of moon-
light on the Sea of Galilee. Jesus bent down to the dirt
and worked up a healing salve from the earth for this
man who had, from birth, missed out on so much of the
beauty of God's good creation.

Jesus spat and rubbed and rolled a mud salve. This
word *salve* suggests to us a kind of ointment that cre-
ates a soothing or healing effect on a wound and is essentially the Latin root of our word *salvation.* It de-
notes a healing, a restored wholeness, wellness. When
I hear or see the word *salve,* I inevitably think of the
little mudpacks we used to make as kids to apply to the
bee stings we occasionally received. Our kid-style ho-
meopathy functioned on the assumption that this little
mud salve, somehow or other, was the best medicine

for a bee's sting. What I hope you will see is that the *salve*-ation God offers us in Jesus Christ is, in fact, a *salving*, a healing, of our whole person, of every dimension of our lives—spiritual, mental, emotional, relational, physical, everything!—in the hope that all of God's good creation can be healed. This is why Charles Wesley has taught us to pray in one of his hymns, "And new-create the world of grace in all the image of Thy love."[6]

How does God "new-create" our lives, and creation as a whole? We believe that God has done, and is doing, this through Jesus Christ. *Jesus himself, the Word who became flesh and lived among us,* is the Salve, the Healing Balm, that God has applied and is applying to our sin-sick world. If we really believe that Jesus is our window into seeing what God is like, and seeing how God labors in the world, then we can affirm with confidence that God is a *Salving Power,* that God's desire is to heal and restore each of us to rich lives of great joy and deep love. "I came," said Jesus, "that they may have life, and have it abundantly" (John 10:10).

But why, we might ask with some justification, did Jesus use a mud salve made from spit to heal this man's blindness? Couldn't He simply have said, "Eyes, be opened"? If we assume He could have done so, then we're really forced to wonder why He didn't. Allow me to suggest some possibilities.

First, we know that in a great many cultures of the ancient world, spit was believed to possess healing pow-

ers. (I know: gross.) It is not impossible that Jesus uti-
lized this method because people could understand it
and maybe even expected it; perhaps the blind man
himself, though unable to see Jesus bent down there in
the dirt, could tell what He was doing or perhaps was
told—so that Jesus' act of making the salve would in
fact raise the man's expectations, would encourage a
hope and faith that were in some way instrumental to
his healing. How many times, after all, did Jesus tell a
person, "Your faith has made you whole"? It is certainly
clear that Jesus got the man quite involved in the whole
process by sending him to the pool of Siloam to wash
off the mud, after which, in John's words, "[he] . . .
came home seeing" (John 9:7, NIV). What if the man
had said instead, "This is ridiculous. You've put mud in
my eyes and now want me to go to the pool and wash it
out. Like this is *gonna help?*" Would he have received
the gift of sight? The man's willingness to "go along
with it," to trust Jesus and obey, was a necessary ingre-
dient in the healing salve Jesus was molding.

We could probably make a fruitful comparison to
baptism at this point; some people think it's just plain
goofy and embarrassing to get all wet in front of everybody, and insist, "After all, what really counts is the
spiritual truth of salvation, so why do I need to get bap-
tized?" Perhaps the best reply is, "I don't know—why
not go ask the man who had mudpacks on his eyes and
was told to go wash them out in the public watering
hole?" In both cases, certainly one of the truths we

would encounter is that salvation is *not* simply spiritual but also physical, not only interior but also out here in the world, not just personal but also social and visible. In this very physical act of washing mud from his eyes, this man demonstrated a measure of faith, a willingness to obey, that brought about both physical and spiritual sight. Even as the man began to see physically, so also his spiritual eyesight sharpened: he moves from simply describing his healer as "the man called Jesus" (9:11) to calling Him "a prophet" (v. 17), to describing Him as a man "from God" (v. 33), to confessing Him, finally, to be "Lord" (v. 38) and Messiah ("Son of Man," vv. 35-36).

Even when we look at the story in this way, we find what we could call a *bent-down healing*. Even if Jesus' spit were nothing more than an accommodation to the way people thought about healing back then, He was still willing to do it that way—to enter into this man's world, so to speak, in order to offer him sight. And again, Jesus would be taking the bent-down approach by getting the man involved in the very process of healing, telling him to go and wash his eyes. There is something significant—in John's term, something of a sign—in the fact that Jesus does not simply issue a command from on high that the man's eyes start seeing, right this instant.

I suggest that we can take this bent-down story a little further. For here we see a Jesus who is quite familiar with the elements of the natural world, with the dirt and spit and stuff of God's creation. He uses His own spit, the dry Palestinian soil, and the waters of Siloam to fashion this man's healing salve. Too often we imagine a Jesus whose head is in the clouds and whose feet are never closer to the ground than 6 or 8 inches. This Jesus kind of glides around with a heavenly glaze in His gaze and is never really in touch with this world of dirt and rocks, water and trees, blue skies and seas, bugs and camels and flowers. *Wrong.* Remember how Jesus taught: Consider the lilies of the field; look at the birds up there in the sky; feel the sunshine on your face; taste the rain and be assured of God's great love for all people. Here is a Messiah who is bent down, who scoops up some dust, spits into it, rolls it around in His rough carpenter hands, and smears it into these poor blind eyes. Obviously, Jesus is not so heavenly, not so spiritual, that He is put off by the nitty-gritty, dirty-spitty elements of earthly existence. Certainly Jesus is not too spiritual to get down into the dirt of your life and mine.

Reuben Welch tells the story of being the preacher in a revival where, after one of the services, a woman new to the church began to unload on him about all the horrible things that had happened in her life the previous few years: spousal abuse and abandonment, larger family squabbles, illness and accidents and deaths.

Finally Reuben asked, "Sister, have you ever gone out at night under the stars and just poured all this out to God?"

"Oh, preacher," she answered, "there are some things that you just don't tell God!"

This woman really needed to see Jesus down there on His knees, spitting in the dirt, didn't she? If Jesus really is the Word, "very God of very God," who became flesh—and blood and bones—and lived among us; if this Incarnate Word could bend down to the ground and spit in the dirt, make a mud salve, smear it on those eyes; if Jesus could live that close to the earth, is it really the case that there are some things that you just don't tell God? I think not.

This bent-down healing also suggests to us that the distinction some people make between spiritual healing and medical healing is poor theology. All healing comes from God our Maker and Molder, and whenever and wherever there is a restoration of health in any measure, we should see in that salving the hand of Christ the Great Physician and give thanks. Some people believe that to seek the wisdom and aid of medicine and doctors is an affront to God, or a sign of no faith; they think that healing can or should come only directly from God, only in a purely spiritual way. This is the heresy, for example, of the Church of Christ, Scientist (i.e., Christian Science). But such apparently superspiritual ideas are an affront to the God who has created us as physical creatures within a physical environment that God has pronounced to be *good*. Jesus, on His knees making a mudpack, is a wonderful bent-down reminder of the *earthiness* of God. As one of the psalms puts it, "He knows how we were made; he remembers that we are dust" (103:14). Because we are made from dust, our ultimate healing, our Great Salve, is God the Word entering into dust and becoming dust with us and among us. Jesus is God's Healing Salve for our bodies and souls.

This brings us to our final consideration. Our understandable tendency not to think of Jesus' healings in such bent-down ways as involving dirt and spit and washing of water is because way too often in the church we have actually become *too spiritual*. What I mean by this is that we think that to become good Christians means that we will try to forget that we are real bodies in a real world of bodies; we will instead think that we should think of ourselves as spirits who just cannot wait to leave the body behind and slip off to heaven. That idea has way more in common with Socrates and Plato than it does with the Bible. We should not forget that the very Gospel that provides the source of our bent-down reflections begins with a radical affirmation of the Word who was God becoming flesh, entering as a real human being into our ailing world.

I remember when I was probably 9 or 10 years old, walking down snow-covered Juniper Street with my tomboy friend Heidi Chambers in the dusk of a wintry December day, Christmas nearing. I prided myself, sadly, on my superior theological training in Sunday School and generally tended to view Heidi as an ignorant pagan. I distinctly recall, in that spirit of superiority, quizzing Heidi as we sludged through the snow, "So, Heidi, do you know what Christmas is all about?"

I will also never forget Heidi's reply: "Ummm . . . isn't it when God got married?"

"Ha! You idiot!"—or something to that effect—was my smart-aleck response. (I worked hard to earn my boyhood nickname of "Know-It-All Lodahl.") It was not till about 25 years later that, as I mulled over Heidi's hesitant answer way back when, it finally dawned on me. *Heidi was right. I made fun of her, but she was right and neither of us knew it.* For in Christmas we who are Christians do in fact rejoice in God's "marriage," so to speak: God becoming united with His own creation in a radical, irreversible way. *And the Word became flesh and lived among us* (John 1:14). That is the miracle and the mystery of the Incarnation—and that is the greatest bent-down story ever told. For the bottom line of our Christian faith is this: There is a balm, a divine healing salve, for each of us and for the world—and His name is *Jesus.*

John 13:3

JESUS, KNOWING THAT THE FATHER
HAD GIVEN ALL THINGS INTO
HIS HANDS . . .

Bent Down— to Wash Feet

I've walked the dusty paths of Jerusalem during the sweltering summer month of July, in sandals no less, so I can testify to just how smelly, sandy, grimy, and gritty those toes can get. It's not a pleasant experience, especially for other folk within smelling range.

So how is it that, on this eve of holy Passover, Jesus and His 12 disciples could shuffle into this little room for supper, smelly feet and all, and ignore the basin filled with water and the servant's towel that must have been right there, over in the corner? Maybe they were hoping a servant would show up and give their tired toes that nice, refreshing bath. Really, according to the custom of the day, whoever served as their host should have supplied the foot washing servant—but the longer they waited, the more aware they became of the sand between their toes and the pebbles in their sandals. The aroma was probably not entirely conducive to fine dining either.

Perhaps they shot glances at each other around the table, everyone with the same thought: "Who, *me?* Surely you don't expect *me* to wash feet! I'm one of the Rabbi's most important disciples! Why, I'm on the church board! There's no way I'm going to do *that!*" It seems likely that Jesus was picking up on those mental signals. It is possible, after all, that this was all Jesus' doing; while the text does not explicitly say so, it would appear that Jesus had set up this entire scenario. Perhaps, Jesus had instructed their host to give the servant the night off—prime time for a lesson in love.

What a scene: the disciples are eating the evening meal, perhaps shooting dirty looks at each other as they wonder just whose feet those are that smell *so* bad. And then there's Jesus: "Jesus, knowing that the Father had given all things into his hands, and that he had come from God and was going to God"—but let's stop right there for just a moment. Let this sink in. The Father had put all things into Jesus' hands, for heaven's sake! He had come from God! He was returning to God! You'd think in this moment Jesus could have done pretty much whatever He wanted. No display of power, might, and authority would have been beyond His capability.

When I was a boy, one of my TV heroes, way back in the black-and-white days, was Superman. I loved Superman. What power! No one could stop him (as long as he kept his distance from kryptonite, of course). Superman was my model for what *real power* is all about. I still remember the narrator voice-over at the beginning of each program: "Faster than a speeding bullet! More powerful than a locomotive! Able to leap tall buildings in a single bound! Look! It's a bird! It's a plane! No, it's *Superman!*" I think I would have assumed, as a little Sunday Schooler fan of Superman, that all Jesus was missing was the red cape. "Faster than a Roman spear! More powerful than an army of those Roman oppressors! Able to leap from the Temple without spraining His ankles!"

But no. John writes instead that Jesus knew that "the Father had given all things into his hands, and that he had come from God and was going to God"—*and so,* precisely for that reason, He got up from the meal, took off His outer cloak, wrapped a towel around His waist, and *bent down on His knees* to wash His disciples' feet. Some versions, such as the *New International,* translate the Greek text to say that "the Father had put all things under his power," and while this is certainly an acceptable equivalent way to put it, it misses what I believe is a crucial point. John writes, literally, that the Father put all things into Jesus' *hands*—and with those very same hands Jesus washed 24 smelly, gritty feet, 2 of which belonged to Judas Iscariot. All this power and authority in His hands—and Jesus exercises this power in a radical expression of humble servanthood that includes even His betrayer. Later in the evening that same Judas, clean feet and all, walked out of that room on his clean feet and into the night to betray Jesus. Jesus was bent down even before Judas.

Like Jesus bending down to scrawl in the dirt or Jesus bending down to make a mudpack salve from dirt and spit, here is yet another bent-down story of Jesus. The very Word of God become flesh and blood and bone was reclining in that room. John wrote earlier in this same Gospel that, while no one has ever seen God, nonetheless "it is God the only Son, who is close to the Father's heart, who has made him known" (1:18). *Jesus had made God known—to us!* Here is the One nearest God's own heart, the One who has come from God and who reveals God's very character, and what is He doing? He's bending down, washing feet like the lowest and most common of servants. I believe that John the apostle would say to us, "Look! That's a portrait of God! That is God washing human feet."

Jesus, on His knees, all power from the Father in His hands, and with those hands He gently washes His disciples' feet—could it really be that this is the very heartbeat of the Maker of the universe? And those very hands would soon be nailed onto a Roman cross. We talk a great deal in our society about upward mobility, and, of course, everyone wants to be upwardly mobile. That's power, that's visibility, that's wealth! But what strikes me about Jesus, time and again, is His amazing gift for downward mobility. You may recall that the apostle Paul puts it this way in Phil. 2: Christ, *being in the very form or nature of God, emptied himself* and became a human servant, humbling himself even to the point of death on a Roman cross (vv. 6-8, author's translation). Can we really believe that this act reveals God—that the Word who was with God and was God and who became flesh and lived among us, is the true unveiling of God's own being, God's own character, God's own love? That would mean that Jesus' life is not some kind of glaring exception to the way God normally is or usually operates; instead, it would mean that it is God's very nature to be humble, to be a servant, to give of himself for our sakes. Thinking of God in that way does not come naturally—which is one of the big reasons why Jesus came. Thinking of ourselves in that way does not come naturally—which is another reason why Jesus came. This really is downward mobility, and that's a direction that most of us have little natural interest in pursuing.

And when Jesus had finished this most menial of tasks, it strikes me as significant that no one in the room said, "Uh, Rabbi, . . . ummm, allow me to wash Your feet." Nobody volunteered—maybe they were all in shock over what Jesus had done! But neither did Jesus say, "Hey! Come on, guys! I did yours, now somebody do Mine." Jesus did not insist that now the disciples owed Him in some way or that from now on they'd be washing His feet. Jesus did, however, point them to each other, just as He now points us to each other in the church, and says to us: "Now that I, your Lord and Teacher, have washed your feet, you also should wash one another's feet" (13:14, NIV).

I think we need to hear this message of John's Gospel. Jesus is forever saying things like, "This is my commandment, that you love one another as I have loved you" (15:12), and "if I . . . have washed your feet, you also ought to wash one another's feet" (13:14). Sometimes in our worship it seems as though we think Jesus actually said things like "Love me as I have loved you," or "Since I have washed your feet, you also ought to wash My feet." We turn Christian discipleship into a personalized, individualized devotion to Jesus; we even sing sometimes that "it's all about" Jesus. If I hear Jesus correctly in the Gospel of John, however, Jesus must be answering something like, "Well, no, it's not all about Me; I'm directing you to love and serve and care for one another." Of course we ought to direct our love and devotion toward Christ, but let us take seriously that Jesus called 12 disciples to become the beginning of a new community, a new fellowship, a new people of God. In other words, Christian faith, Christian devotion, and Christian practice all happen in and happen as a community of disciples. Jesus calls us to wash one another's feet.

Gayle Erwin is an old friend of mine, a pastoral colleague and mentor when I was just starting in pastoral ministry in the Los Angeles area over 20 years ago. During that era he wrote a book called *The Jesus*

Style that, I can happily report, was actually the style that characterized Erwin's life and ministry back then —and still does today. In that book he comments wisely on this text:

> Had it been me, I would have held one foot slightly elevated for all the disciples to see as I coughed nervously and hinted that something important had been left undone. It would have been beneath me to do such work.
>
> Peter recognized that this behavior was beneath the dignity of Jesus. He was unable to receive such a free gift so he told Jesus he would not allow his feet to be washed. Jesus' answer speaks volumes about our relationship to him and each other, and about his nature. "Unless I wash you, you have no part with me." Unless we understand the true nature of Jesus and let him be to us what he is to be, we can never fully comprehend him or truly be a part of him.[7]

This "true nature of Jesus" is the servant nature. I think we generally understand and believe this. But I think we also often suspect that it was just a temporary ruse, that if Jesus really is God, then the next time around Jesus certainly will be different! This is where we truly need to hear John's message again: "The Word was with God, and the Word was God" (1:1). The life and ministry of Jesus really do provide *the Revelation of God*. Thus, Jesus the Servant must truly reveal that God, the very God of all creation, is a Servant. This is why, when "the Father had given all things into his hands" (13:3), what Jesus did with those power-filled hands was to wash feet. This is why to be godly, to be godlike, is to be a servant. It is to live in the fellowship of Jesus' disciples as one who serves—and as one who is served. We are called to the grace both of giving to and receiving from one another. Erwin continues:

> Peter's response [to Jesus] is typical of the way we approach one another. "Above all, you must not see the real me," we reason. "I will wash my own feet and you can rinse them ritually." Perhaps, just as not letting Jesus wash our feet removes us from fellowship with him, not fulfilling the command of Jesus to wash one another's feet removes us from fellowship with each other. We are to be cleansing agents to each other, removing the dust of our daily travels to prepare us to sit at the Lord's table.[8]

Jesus does indeed point us to one another, to our fellow travelers, to those in whose company and encouragement we live our discipleship to Jesus Christ. "I have set you an example, that you also should do as I have done to you" (v. 15). Do we wash one another's feet? Do we bear one another's burdens? Or do we often just heap more junk on the shoulders of our fellow travelers? Do we kick up a little more dust, make the journey a little more grimy for one another way too often? Are we able and willing to stoop down and wash someone's feet?

When I think about this commandment of Jesus, I generally do not think it was meant literally—I *can't* think that, since I have so rarely washed someone else's feet! It's interesting how we decide which passages should be taken literally in the Bible; this one has not tended to get many votes. Yet we really have little reason to assume Jesus did not mean for us to practice this command literally. "If you know these things," Jesus adds after insisting that His disciples wash one another's feet, "you are blessed if you do them" (v. 17).

One of the few times my feet have been washed by a fellow disciple of Jesus occurred during my seminary days. I was a regular attendee at Blue Hills Church of the Nazarene in Kansas City, a predominantly African-American congregation in which I and a few other seminary students and spouses were the only white folk. During one Sunday night service the pastor, Larry Lott, was doing something entirely unexpected by us in the pews. While we sang hymns and spirituals, Pastor Lott was calling up people from the congregation, one by one, to the pulpit loft area. He was washing their feet.

I remember sitting in that church that night, just praying and hoping that Pastor Lott would not call my name. I slouched down low in the pew. I gauged the distance to the nearest exit: no good, it was too far away, with too many rows of pews to navigate gracefully. I wanted to be invisible. But apparently I wasn't; suddenly I heard him calling my name. "Mike. Brother Mike Lodahl. Come on up here."

Oh, I did not want this! I did not want my pastor —a man whom I loved and admired so deeply, a man from whom I had learned so much about being a shepherd of God's people—to wash my feet. I especially did not want him, a black man, to be bending low at my feet, the feet of a white man, to perform such a menial task. I did not like the symbolism of the black man as my servant. I wanted to run out of the church.

But I didn't. I got up from my place in the pew and trudged up toward the front of the church while the singing continued. Maybe if I walked slowly enough, Jesus would come back before I'd get there and Pastor Lott wouldn't have to wash my feet after all.

That didn't happen. And so I sat before a kneeling Larry Lott—man of God, powerful preacher, caring pastor. I sat helplessly and watched as he lovingly removed my shoes, then my socks—oh please, not my socks—and began ever so gently to wash my feet. I felt so uncomfortable, so not in control. Yet I must testify: as Pastor Lott washed my feet, I began to feel loved by God in a way I never had before and never have since. God's love washed over me like a gentle flood. I was bathed in love divine, all loves excelling. Could it be that I was indeed experiencing the *power* of God? Yes, indeed.

I have been wondering recently what kind of Christian congregations would develop from the practice of foot washing. What kind of disciples would be formed, over an extended period of time, among people who actually, literally practiced Jesus' command? I don't have an answer; I've just been wondering. But I do know this: Servanthood doesn't have to be the big splashy effect, even if foot washing can't help but be a little splashy. But perhaps there are other ways to wash one another's feet. Perhaps it will be a simple smile or word of encouragement that will wash away some of the cares and anxieties of the week. Maybe it will involve sacrificing a little of our fine-tuned schedules in order simply to lend an ear to someone who's struggling. For my wife, Janice, and me, one way over the years that we have quietly attempted to serve one another in a small way is to put the toothpaste on each other's brush. It's taking servanthood one step beyond refraining from complaining about how she squeezes from the middle of the tube. It's no big deal, of course, to squeeze a little bit of toothpaste onto your loved one's toothbrush. We do not treat it as a rigid rule at all, but rather more as an occasional token of our love. But when I go to the bathroom sink and see the toothpaste already squeezed onto my toothbrush, I feel loved and cared for. It doesn't always take the huge effort to *bend down.*

The point is that Jesus demonstrated the very heart and character of God Almighty, Maker of the heavens and the earth, by getting on His knees like the lowest of servants and washing feet. He was not behaving contrary to the heart of God; He was revealing, even expressing, the heart of God. So when Jesus then in turn calls us, His followers, to live in servanthood with one another, He is calling us to lives that truly reflect what God is like. The God we serve is a Servant—in fact, *the Servant!* Anglican theologian John Macquarrie wrote a little book called *The Humility of God* that explores this very theme. Ask the average Joe or Josephine on the street what God is like, and you're very likely to hear adjectives like *almighty* and *powerful* and *all-knowing.* Perhaps someone will mention *loving.* But few would connect God's loving quality with a heart of humble servanthood. But we who are Christians should!—for "no one has ever seen God. It is God the only Son, who is close to the Father's heart, who has made him known" (1:18).

Perhaps it is even divine humility that leads Jesus to say to His disciples, "So if I . . . have washed your feet, you also ought to wash one another's" (13:14), instead of drawing attention back to himself. Perhaps this is why Jesus says, "As I have loved you, you also should love one another" (v. 34). Notice again how Jesus does not say, "As I have loved you, so you are to love Me." Jesus directs us to each other, especially to one another in the local church congregation, to love as He loves; in fact, He goes on to lay down this acid test: "By this everyone will know that you are my disciples, if you have love for one another" (v. 35).

But remember that it is not just a matter of being the foot washer—we are each called also to be a washee! Jesus said to wash one another's feet, to love one another. Each of us is one of those "one anothers," which means that you and I must be willing to be on the receiving end as well as on the giving end. The fact is that for some of us, it is actually easier to be the giver, the servant, the one who loves, because at least then we still feel as if we're in control. But to let someone else love and serve us—like Jesus insisted of Peter—means we're no longer really in control. We're vulnerable, our lives kind of opened up—especially when we are revealing our weird toes or smelly feet to someone else! Further, many of us often feel that we really do not deserve to be loved or cared for or served anyway. But the Church exists to extend the love of God in Jesus Christ to all—which includes you and me.

All this must mean that Jesus Christ is looking to create in each of our local church congregations a true *fellowship* (the Greek word is *koinonia*), a common life of mutual sharing. In such a fellowship, the disciples of Jesus give love and receive love; they reach out to others and allow others to touch them in return; they share and also benefit from the sharing of others; they wash feet and let their feet be washed. May all who confess Christ as Lord become downwardly mobile, bent-down people in the name and foot-washing power of Jesus.

So I ask: Washed any feet lately? Or let someone else wash yours?

John 21:12

JESUS SAID TO THEM,
"COME AND HAVE BREAKFAST."

A Bent-Down Breakfast

CHAPTER FOUR

It was one of the most amazing experiences of my half-century of life. Back in July of 1986, I was privileged to spend the month studying in Jerusalem and traveling throughout Israel on the weekends. My colleagues and I would work hard during the week studying with professors from Hebrew University, and then on weekends we'd play hard. One weekend we all headed northeast from Jerusalem up into the region of Galilee. It was a *hot* day, and in the middle of that sweltering afternoon our little van emptied out its sweltering passengers at a resort town called Tiberias on the western shore of the Sea of Galilee. Most of us changed into our swimming suits as quickly as we could—and then charged off the pier into Galilee's fresh, refreshing waters. The water was so cool and inviting, I just had to swallow a few gulpfuls; since for the first time in my life I was in the Sea of Galilee (a freshwater lake, of course), it only seemed right that a little of the Sea of Galilee should be in me.

As I swam that afternoon, just taking in the sun and water and happy voices of my fellow students, something began very gradually to dawn on me. I still remember, almost as though with each stroke I took, how the pieces began to fall into place. I recalled that the final chapter of John's Gospel tells us that Jesus appeared to His disciples this third time by the Sea of Tiberias. Here I was, swimming in the Sea of Galilee— and in a couple of strokes I remembered that the Sea of Tiberias was another name for the Sea of Galilee. Maybe John meant by "the Sea of Tiberias" that this appearance of Jesus occurred right here in the region of Tiberias. This resort where we were swimming was on the same site where the ancient town of Tiberias had once been. Another stroke or two, and it was dawning on me that I was swimming in the same waters where Peter had swum! Perhaps it was *right here,* at this point in the Sea of Galilee nearly 2,000 years ago, that Peter had swum ashore that misty morning be- cause he knew *Jesus,* raised from the dead, was there waiting for him on the rocky beach.

As I floated on my back out there in those invigor- ating waters, I had to wonder, as so many have before me, why Peter and his friends had gone fishing. Not that there's necessarily anything wrong with fishing! But somehow it just seems like a strange way for Peter to deal with the resurrection of Jesus. After all, Jesus had already appeared to His disciples twice before and had even breathed upon them with these words, "Receive the Holy Spirit" (John 20:22). Yet apparently these followers of Jesus were still struggling with what they should be doing with themselves, a bit unsure about what was to happen next. There's just something so matter-of-fact, so plain and vaguely disappointing about Peter making the announcement, "I'm going fishing." It sounds a bit like a concession on Peter's part, as though he were simply going back to life as usual, back to the nets and boats and fish that he'd been willing to leave behind when Jesus had called him, "Follow me" (1:43), several years earlier. Now it's like a period of limbo: a lack of direction, perhaps even boredom, that has set in on Peter and a half dozen of the other disciples—including Thomas, the doubter, who had already touched (or at least had been invited to touch!) the wounds of the living, resurrected Christ. *So why were they going fishing?*

Nothing wrong with it, of course. Maybe they were just hungry! Perhaps there were bills to be paid.

One thing is certain. When Peter was out in that boat, he was in what we call nowadays his comfort zone. This was his territory, his domain. Out there in that boat he was back in control; out there he felt secure. For three years he had been out of his element, like a fish—or a fisherman!—out of water. He had followed this Carpenter from Nazareth, had seen Him heal the sick and cast out demons, had heard Him

teach with power and authority, had watched Him weep
with compassion and laugh with joy, had witnessed Him
touching lepers and eating with tax collectors. Peter
had confessed that this One was the Messiah and had
heard Jesus' response of blessing upon him. But he had
also tried to talk Jesus out of this crazy idea about getting crucified and had been called a devil. He had followed Jesus all the way into Jerusalem and felt the joy-
ful anticipation of the crowds that welcomed Jesus. But
he had also been there later that very same week, the
night Jesus was arrested, the night Jesus had bent
down and washed his feet. Then the next day he had
watched with agony as Jesus was nailed to a Roman
cross.

But worst of all, he now lived with the shame and
self-condemnation of having denied Jesus three times
in one night. He had called Jesus his Teacher and Lord
for three years and then had flushed it all away in the
matter of one cold evening. Peter had been on an emotional roller coaster for three years—a wild ride where
he never knew what was coming next—and when you've
been on the roller coaster that long, time comes when
you just have to get off. And Peter did: "I'm going fishing." There's pain in that declaration. There's some
resignation there. But there is also a return to the rela-
tive comfort, security, and predictability of his boats
and sails and nets. This he could handle.

Quite possibly, too, Peter felt sure that even
though Jesus had appeared to him and the other disci-

ples, he had failed so miserably that there was no way Jesus had any use for him now. He had made such big promises, like "Even if everyone else deserts you, I never will" (Matt. 26:33, NLT). Yet for all his talk, when the pressure was on, he didn't walk the walk. How could Jesus ever really use him now?

So Peter went back to the old life. But wouldn't you know it: his first night back to the old boats, and they didn't catch a thing. The fish just were not biting. And at the end of that long and frustrating night, in the misty, murky morning haze, he and his exhausted friends could make out an indistinct figure ambling along the shore.

"Hey, guys, you caught anything."

"No!"

"Well, try throwing your nets over on the other side of the boat."

This was all starting to feel a little familiar. Indeed, according to Luke's Gospel, just such an encounter as this marked the first meeting between Jesus and Peter several years back (Luke 5:1-11). I suspect about now Peter began to feel that, in the inimitable phrase of that master wordsmith Yogi Berra, this was "déjà vu all over again." When they slung those nets over to the other side and came up with a huge, swarming catch, that was the clincher. Peter and John both knew who the Stranger on the shore was. Peter, big kid that he was, just couldn't wait to come ashore with everyone else. No, he had to jump in and swim for all he was worth.

And now I swam in those very waters.

Later that evening my friends and I enjoyed Friday night Sabbath dinner at a restaurant perched right on that same shore, overlooking the waters of Galilee. We all ordered the specialty of the house—"St. Peter's Fish," it's called—complete with tail and head, eyeballs and all. Good as it was, I think our cook was pretty normal. Our waiter, while certainly polite and helpful, was nothing out of the ordinary.

But what about the *real* "St. Peter's fish"? Peter and those six fellow disciples had an amazing and utterly unique breakfast. For on the shore, *bent down* tending a little charcoal fire cooking fish and toasting bread—*there was Jesus!* Is this not simply an amazing portrait of the resurrected Lord and King of Kings? He is bending down low to the ground, yet again, this time to *cook breakfast* for His tired and hungry friends—the friends who had abandoned and disowned Him. But here He is anyway, the Lord Jesus down there in that rocky sand, the waters of Galilee lapping peacefully on the shore, and He's poking hot coals with a stick. And I have to ask: *Is this any way for a resurrected Lord, the Son of God, to behave?* And we should answer, Apparently it is!

"Come and have some breakfast," He says.

Jesus is no different today, is He? "Jesus Christ is the same yesterday and today and forever" (Heb. 13:8). The living Christ cares for you and me; He invites us to warm up at the fire, and yearns to feed us, to nourish us, to strengthen and encourage us. "Come and have breakfast." In the words of the old camp meeting favorite, reprinted in full at the end of this chapter: *Come and dine, the Master calleth, Come and dine.*

It is interesting that John adds the somewhat odd observation that "none of the disciples dared to ask him, 'Who are you?' because they knew it was the Lord" (21:12). We might wonder, Could there have been any doubt about it? But we should also recall that the resurrected Christ apparently was not always immediately recognizable (Luke 24:15-16; John 20:11-16). We may assume that Jesus' resurrection appearances were marked by a sense of great mystery, even some eeriness (Luke 24:36-39). *Is this really our Teacher, the very man who was crucified?* But as Jesus invited His weary friends to breakfast by the fire on this marvelous morn, there were no doubts about the identity of their Host. They knew it was the Lord who was their Servant. John continues, "Jesus came and took the bread and gave it to them"—*I really think Jesus likes passing out bread, don't you?*—"and did the same with the fish" (John 21:13). Yes, they knew it was the Lord, and it was precisely as *their Lord and ours* that the resurrected Jesus cooked breakfast—a bent-down breakfast. He broke the bread and served them all, offering himself to them yet again in kind and humble love. Jesus always lived what He taught, never asking His disciples to do anything that He himself was not willing to do. So now, once more, and even as the resurrected Lord of heaven and earth, He continues not only on that morning but even today to be a Servant—*the* Servant of all. It is mind-blowing that even in His resurrection glory Jesus is still a servant, a bent-down Lord.

Then there is Peter. Think of it: he had denied Jesus three times while standing near a charcoal fire to keep warm through the night of his Master's arrest (18:18). Now he warms himself by another charcoal fire, almost as though it were the re-creation of the scene of denial. Now, even as Jesus offers warmth and nourishment to Peter, He also begins to put the question to Peter, to dig beneath the surface, to "deepen the situation" in probing Peter's heart. *Do you love me?* Three times Jesus put this question to Peter—not, I am sure, to humiliate him, but in fact to give him a way back into full fellowship with his Lord. Jesus gave Peter just as many opportunities to affirm his love for Jesus as he'd had to deny even knowing who Jesus was. Jesus, on that cool, misty morning, was giving Peter a way back into His heart, but giving him a path that took seriously the pain and shame of his abandonment and denial. "Do you love me?"

How do we answer Jesus' question, put to us just as surely as it was to Peter? Do we love Him? Do we see that He asks us each that simple question from His bent-down position in the sand, stirring coals with a stick, His eyes looking upward into yours and mine? Who *is* this Lord who looks *upward* to meet our eyes and to embrace our wayward heart? He is the One who loves us with an everlasting love, a love that will not let us go.

If we answer yes to Jesus' question, I cannot imagine that His response to us will be much different from the one He gave to Peter that morning: "Feed my sheep" (v. 17). Take care of My little ones. Feed and nurture My little lambs. Jesus had already demonstrated this very act by cooking fish and toasting bread on a charcoal fire by the Sea of Galilee, nourishing His tired, hungry, confused disciples. And having loved in this way, He calls Peter, and calls us too, to love in this way. To love Jesus is not simply to love Jesus, period. Rather, to love Jesus is to feed His sheep, to care for His tired and hungry people. Friends, to love Jesus is, finally, to *bend down there with Him,* to tend to the needs of His sheep. That is where Jesus is—and He is asking you and me to join Him.

"'Come and dine,' the Master calleth." This wonderful camp meeting song beautifully weaves imagery of Jesus feeding His shivering disciples by the lakeside with that of the cup and bread of the Lord's Supper— and thus also, finally, with that of the great heavenly banquet in the age to come. *Jesus feeds us.* And then we, too, if we love the One who feeds and nourishes us, are called upon also to call out to the hungry, the cold, the worn, and the discouraged: "Come and dine."

Come and Dine

C. B. Widmeyer

Jesus has a table spread
Where the saints of God are fed;
He invites His chosen people, "Come and dine."
With His manna He doth feed
And supplies our ev'ry need.
O 'tis sweet to sup with Jesus all the time!

Refrain:
"Come and dine," the Master calleth, "come and dine."
You may feast at Jesus' table all the time.
He who fed the multitude, turned the water into wine,
To the hungry calleth now, "Come and dine."

The disciples came to land,
Thus obeying Christ's command;
For the Master called to them, "O come and dine."
There they found their heart's desire—
Bread and fish upon the fire;
Thus He satisfies the hungry ev'ry time.

Soon the Lamb will take His bride
To be ever at His side;
All the host of heaven will assembled be.
O 'twill be a glorious sight—
All the saints in spotless white;
And with Jesus they will feast eternally.

John 14:7

IF YOU KNOW ME, YOU WILL KNOW
MY FATHER ALSO. FROM NOW ON
YOU DO KNOW HIM AND
HAVE SEEN HIM.

"No One Has Ever Seen God"

CHAPTER FIVE

The previous four meditations from the Gospel of John should have made a couple of things obvious. First, John's portrayal of Jesus seems to favor stories in which Jesus is, as we have been putting it, "bent down." After all, none of those four stories is found in any of the other Gospels; all of them are unique to John. Second, John's Gospel more than the other three places a distinct emphasis upon the critical Christian theological principle that the person, words, and works of Jesus truly do reveal the very nature of God.

If we combine these two themes from John's Gospel, the result is likely to be surprising, if not shocking: *the bent-down Jesus is* **the Revelation** *of who God is, and what God is like!* Indeed, we have already considered the wonderful Christian truth that in the Incarnation—the Word who was and is God becoming the human being Jesus of Nazareth and living among us—we encounter the greatest bent-down story ever told. The Incarnation of God in the human person of Jesus is the bent-down movement of our Maker that makes all the other bent-down stories possible.

This is what makes the closing statement of John's prologue (1:1-18) so amazing, so radical. In verse 18, John boldly claims that "No one has ever seen God" and immediately follows with an awfully important "however" statement: "It is God the only Son, who is close to the Father's heart, who has made [God] known."

No one has ever seen God. When I study this passage with university students, the ones who are well-versed (literally!) are quick to bring up Old Testament stories like Adam and Eve, conversing with God in the Garden of Eden; or Moses, who is said to have spoken "face to face" with God (Exod. 33:11); or even the prophet Isaiah, who reported that "in the year that King Uzziah died, I saw the Lord sitting on a throne, high and lofty" (Isa. 6:1). With passages like these, how could the Gospel of John ever make such a categorical statement as "No one has ever seen God"?

This is a good question—and I continue to believe that what makes a good question is that it is better than any answer one might give to it! After all, it is not possible that John did not know those Old Testament stories. He surely did. But it seems to me he is trying to say that, in comparison with the revelation we have received in the Word who "became flesh and lived among us" (John 1:14), those stories just cannot compare. Further, "No one has ever seen God" is certainly about far more than whether anyone has ever seen God with human eyes. Indeed, we read in Exodus that God's word to Moses was "no one shall see me and live" (33:20). Perhaps John's point is that no one has really comprehended or apprehended God; no one has really had a handle on the Holy Mystery who is our Creator. In this way of thinking about it, "No one has ever seen God" would mean that God is not an object of human perception, understanding, or observation. "No one has ever seen God" would remind us that we human beings, even at our best, are still only finite, frail creatures of dust whose Creator is infinitely beyond our capacities to imagine.

You would probably have to be at least my age to remember the Russian cosmonaut who, in the early 1960s, made several orbits around planet Earth and then returned safely to his motherland. When he was safe and sound and ready to provide sound bites, one of his announcements to the press was that in his great space journey beyond earth's atmosphere, he had seen no God up there.

Looking back, I now suppose that, as much as anything else, this was a little slice of communist propaganda. But I recall that, as a boy of five or six at the time, I was more than a little disconcerted by this cosmonaut's announcement. As the little theologian-in-the-making that I was, I wished that the cosmonaut had gotten at least a glimpse of the Almighty up there and had returned to the planet as a true believer—or at least had brought back some assurance about God's reality for the rest of us!

But he did not—and what I did not understand then is that the opening of John's Gospel already offered assurances that God, in principle, is not visible to the human eye. God is not an object of perception or examination. We do not hold God at arm's length, turning God at various angles to get the best view. Blasting off in a rocket will not get us a closer perspective. We cannot manipulate God according to our whim, nor even imagine God in heavenly glory with our eyes closed in religious ecstasy. Neither the most powerful telescope, nor the most meticulous of microscopes, could draw God into our line of vision. God simply is not an object among other objects, like people and trees and stars and butterflies. God is *God*—the Creator "who gives life to all things," who alone "has immortality and dwells in unapproachable light, whom no one has ever seen or can see" (1 Tim. 6:13, 16).

However.

And that is where Jesus comes in. "It is God the only Son, who is close to the Father's heart, who has made him known" (John 1:18). Without Jesus, John is saying, we would be totally blind when it comes to God. We would be clueless. This is why, later in this

Gospel, Jesus would say to His disciples, "Whoever has seen me has seen the Father" (14:9). Jesus was not claiming to *be* the Father—that is something Jesus never does—but that as His disciples watched Him in action and listened to His words, they were recipients of the Father's self-revelation. "Do you not believe that I am in the Father and the Father is in me?" He added (v. 10). His entire ministry was a full-orbed, flesh-and-blood answer to Philip's request of Jesus, "Lord, show us the Father, and we will be satisfied" (v. 8).

This, then, is what makes those bent-down stories of Jesus in the Gospel of John so revolutionary. When, for example, Jesus knelt to wash His disciples' feet, He was in the Father and the Father was in Him! So it was that Jesus, "knowing that the Father had given all things into his hands" (13:3), immediately put those hands to the servile work of washing dirty, smelly toes. Further, it was directly following the foot washing incident that Jesus said to Philip and the rest of the disciples, "If you know me, you will know my Father also. From now on you do know him and have seen him" (14:7). Is it possible that Jesus' phrase *from now on* refers specifically to this supreme act of servanthood that had just occurred—His washing of those two dozen feet? Was Jesus saying that it was specifically in that act, as in no other act, that the disciples "have seen" God the Father whom "no one has ever seen"? It is at the very least a tantalizing possibility.

In any event, there is no way around it: God the

Father is a bent-down God. This really is the unavoidable conclusion to the bent-down stories of Jesus we have been mulling over in the first half of this little book.

Now we prepare to embark on the second half. In the four chapters that are to follow, we will contemplate passages from the letters of John as complements to the Gospel stories of the first four chapters. While there are no bent-down stories, as such, in those letters, we will find plenty of instruction for Jesus' disciples, the Church, that will make it clear that we are called to be a bent-down people.

There is, in fact, a critical point of connection between the Gospel of John and the letter we call 1 John, a point that really is the heart of this chapter. Interestingly enough, 1 John includes the same, somewhat surprising claim we have been reflecting upon from John 1:18. In 1 John 4:12, we find it: "No one has ever seen God." There it is again. This time, though, the "however" follow-up statement is noticeably different: "No one has ever seen God; if we love one another, God lives in us, and his love is perfected in us." We find, then, that on the one hand John's Gospel teaches that the invisible God is revealed by Jesus; on the other hand, John's first letter teaches that the invisible God is revealed by the Church, the communion of Christian disciples, when they love one another as Jesus has loved them. Truly these two statements of John belong together. John's Gospel sheds beautiful light on the doctrine of Christ, or Christology; John's letters shed beautiful light on the doctrine of the church, or ecclesiology (from the Greek word *ekklēsia,* or "the ones who are called out," consistently translated "church" in the New Testament).

"As the Father has loved me, so I have loved you," Jesus says to us, His disciples (John 15:9). That is very assuredly good news, but it is always only half of the equation; Jesus invariably adds, "Just as I have loved you, you also should love one another" (13:34). This chain reaction of love is the very revelation of God in this world! John's first letter tells us that "God is love" (1 John 4:8, 16), the self-giving love revealed in the living and dying of Jesus (3:16). This love, John writes, continues to be revealed to the world as we love one another as God has loved us. "No one has ever seen God," but God will "look like" your smile offered to the new visitor at church; God will "feel like" your hand extended to someone in need; God will "sound like" your words of encouragement spoken to the one who is struggling. In the second half of this book, then, we will explore how Jesus' disciples are called and empowered to be a bent-down people.

It comes down to this:

No one has ever seen God. *However, there's Jesus.*

No one has ever seen God. *However, there are Jesus' disciples.*

The question is, In the light of the bent-down Jesus, how ought we disciples of Jesus to live?

John 8:8

AND ONCE AGAIN HE BENT DOWN
AND WROTE ON THE GROUND.

God's Word from the Beginning

CHAPTER SIX

The more we reflect upon this portrait of
the bent-down Jesus, the more striking it
all becomes. Remember that a group of
Pharisees were attempting to trap Jesus
in a no-win situation, and that the basis
for their argument was, to use a common
contemporary phrase, "the authority of
the Word." They and Jesus—and undoubtedly the woman, too!—knew that
the Law of Moses was painfully clear on
the issue of adultery. "If a man is caught
lying with the wife of another man, both
of them shall die . . . So you shall purge
the evil from Israel" (Deut. 22:22). It was
all right there in black and white.

What is not in black and white, of
course, is whatever it was that Jesus
scrawled in the sand. We do not know
what Jesus wrote, despite all the well-in-
tentioned guesses of thousands of preachers over 20 centuries. We do not know

what Jesus wrote, or even if He wrote anything. What we do have from this marvelous story, though, is a picture of Jesus bent down, His finger of flesh and blood and bone making its mark in the ground. This page of Scripture offers us no written words from Jesus—but it does offer us a portrait of the Word that "became flesh and lived among us," a Word who could bend all the way down and touch the earth. This is the living Word, the very Word who was with God and who is God, entering deeply into the earthly stuff of creaturely existence. That is where you and I live.

The New Testament document we call 1 John begins by making the very same claim. "We declare to you what was *from the beginning,* what we have heard, what we have seen with our eyes, what we have looked at and touched with our hands, concerning the word of life" (1:1, emphasis added throughout). So far it reads almost like the sequel to the Gospel of John, which begins: *"In the beginning* was the Word, and the Word was with God, and the Word was God. . . . And the Word became flesh and lived among us" (John 1:1, 14). Long before there was the written word of Moses—infinite eternities before—there was this Word, this Logos, that shared in God's very being. No wonder, then, that while John's Gospel concedes that "the law indeed was given through Moses," it immediately proceeds to insist that "grace and *truth* came through Jesus Christ" (v. 17). John follows that somewhat surprising claim with the even more radical statement we considered in the previous chapter, "No one has ever seen God. It is God the only Son, who is close to the Father's heart, who has made him known" (v. 18).

This takes us back to that introduction in 1 John: What was *from the beginning* has come down all the way into our world. The Word of life was heard, was seen, and was touched by those among whom He lived and served. This visible, tangible Word was *from the beginning,* and it is this incarnate Word who has made God known to us. Given this fundamental Christian truth regarding the Incarnation, it is a strange but un-avoidable fact that the bent-down Jesus, in the very act of scribbling in the sand with His touchable finger, was making the invisible God known to us. He is the Word that was from the beginning.

In what follows in this chapter I intend to trace John's repeated use of the phrase *from the beginning,* for I have become convinced that it plays a profound role in what this little letter has to say to Jesus' disci-ples today. "From the beginning," like the Gospel of John's "in the beginning," seems to imply that which is of God—that which is from the very heart of who God is, of what God is like, and of what God desires for the world. Whatever is "from the beginning," we might say, "goes way back" because it flows out of God's own un-fathomable being.

It does not take John long to return to the phrase. "Beloved," he writes in chapter 2, "I am writing you no new commandment, but an old commandment that you have had *from the beginning;* the old commandment is the word that you have heard" (v. 7). Keep in mind how this letter began! "What was from the beginning, what we *have heard*" (1:1). What we have heard from the beginning is the same Word seen by the eyes of the apostles and touched by their hands—the Word of life who "was revealed to us" (v. 2). But now John is adding that this word is itself a commandment—indeed, an "old commandment."

On the other hand, John essentially says, this old commandment actually is a "new commandment"! Why? Because this commandment is "true in him" (2:8)— which apparently means that this commandment has been fulfilled, has been fleshed out, has become incarnate in the person of Jesus. We don't know yet what the commandment is, but we know where to look to see it actually lived! While we are looking at this passage, however, we should probably note that John writes further that this commandment is not only "true in him" (Jesus) but also "in you"—or, to be more precise about the Greek grammar, "in y'all"! Whatever this commandment is that we have had "from the beginning," because it has become "true-ified" (we might say) in Jesus, it can and should also become "true-ified" in and among Jesus' followers. So it is that, just a little later, John counsels us to "let what you heard from the beginning abide in you. If what you heard from the beginning abides in you, then you will abide in the Son and in the Father" (v. 24). John still has not come out and just told us plainly what it is, exactly, that we "have heard from the beginning," but it is becoming increasingly obvious that, whatever it is, it is important.

It isn't until well into the next chapter that we find, precisely and clearly, what this "from the beginning" word or command actually is. "For this is the message you have heard from the beginning, that we should love one another" (3:11). The *from the beginning* Word / Message / Command from the very heart of God is precisely this and nothing other: "love one another." Indeed, we find the identical idea in the little letter called 2 John: "I ask you, not as though I were writing you a new commandment, but one we have had from the beginning, let us love one another" (v. 5).

The implication of this line of thought is remarkable. The letters of John are telling us that the very Word who was with God, and who is God—this Word that became one of us and lived among us as Jesus the Nazarene—this Word is also God's Message, God's Command, to us! God's command to "love one another" is "true in him" because He perfectly and entirely embodied (and embodies) this love.

Take all of this back into the story of Jesus, bent down low to the ground, scribbling in the dirt beside a terrified, humiliated woman and a crowd of men bent on violence. These men could point to the very words on the scroll of Deuteronomy that commanded death for all adulterers. They had it down, "chapter and verse," so to speak. But in Jesus a more fundamental Word, the Message from the beginning, is being true-ified as He bends down to the dirt and probes the very earth we walk on with His finger of flesh, His finger of love. He *is* God's commandment to "love one another." The Law may have come through Moses, but "grace and truth"—God's truth from the beginning—"came through Jesus Christ" (John 1:17).

The Jewish tradition of which the Pharisees were an important part had counted up the divine command-ments in the laws of Moses and had arrived at the daunting number of 613. Rabbis even came up with a clever rationale for this number: along with 365 days in the year, they said, there are 248 bones in the body. Add those two numbers, and you get 613. Thus, they argued, we see that God's commandments cover every bone of our bodies every moment of our lives. No as-pect of life, at any time, is left outside of God's scruti-ny and concern. (Never mind that 248 bones is not anatomically correct; the theological point is what mat-ters!) It was one of those 613 that the Pharisees were waving in Jesus' face in that tense and threatening sit-uation.

Of course, when we read the Synoptic Gospels (Matthew, Mark, and Luke) we repeatedly find Jesus summing up those 613 commands under 2: To love God with our entire being (Deut. 6:4-5) and to love our neighbors as our very selves (Lev. 19:18). Wonderful as those two commands are, as the two upon which all others hang (Matt. 22:40), they are nowhere to be found in John's Gospel or letters. Instead, there we find just this one commandment that, like the 613, omits no aspect of our lives at any moment. This all-embracing commandment is, simply, "that we should love one another" (1 John 3:11). Again, given the message of John, there is a fundamental truth at work here—no matter what Jesus may or may not have written in the dirt in that ugliest of situations, His entire life and ministry was a grand process of "true-ifying" God's command *from the beginning* that we are to love one another.

This revolutionary idea in the writings of John, though, commands our attention even a bit further. We'll start with the second letter of John and work our way back toward John's Gospel for this next consideration. We have already seen that in 2 John 5 the church (in this letter referred to as "the elect lady and her children"; see v. 1) is begged to follow the "new commandment . . . we have had from the beginning, let us love one another" (v. 5). John follows this with the statement, "And this is love, that we walk according to his commandments" (v. 6)—and immediately we would be thrust back, it might appear, to a list (no doubt for us not as long as 613!) of things God commands us to do. In other words, it might be tempting for someone to say, "Aha! All this talk about love, but now John makes it clear that love means following God's commandments." Again, then we would be left with trying to sort out exactly which commandments—if not all of them—John has in mind. Most likely, we would begin with the Ten Commandments and go from there.

However, I believe to do that would be to miss just how radical John's message truly is. Remember again that while "the law [i.e., commandments] indeed was given through Moses; grace and truth came through Jesus Christ" (John 1:17). With that in mind, we return to 2 John 6, where we have just read that love is "that we walk according to his commandments." *Immediately* John adds, "This is the commandment, as you have heard it *from the beginning,* that you follow love" (2 John 6, RSV). The commandments of God have become the commandment, just like that. The logic gets a little tangled, yet the point is simple: We have had a commandment from the beginning, that we love one another. To love is to follow God's commandments, and there is but one: Follow the way of love.

Lest we should think that this is some kind of fluke or idiosyncrasy in John's writings, we now move to his first letter. There we read that "we have boldness before God; and we receive from him whatever we ask, because we obey his commandments and do what pleases him" (1 John 3:21-22). What does John immediately write next? "And this is his commandment, that we should believe in the name of his Son Jesus Christ and love one another, just as he has commanded us" (v. 23)! Again, God's commandments have become God's commandment—even in this case, where it seems John lists two commands. But this is the point, and it is a profound one: to believe in God's Son Jesus Christ is absolutely, positively inseparable from loving one another in Jesus' circle of followers. There is but one commandment—indeed, a commandment we have heard from the beginning—and it is to love one another just as Jesus both embodied and commanded.

John was on solid gospel ground in reducing God's commands to a single command; after all, this fascinating shift is found also in his Gospel. There, in chapter 15, we find Jesus addressing His disciples (including you and me) with His analogy of the vine and the branches. Let us isolate and follow the steps of logic in this passage:

- "Abide in me as I abide in you" (v. 4).
- "Those who abide in me and I in them bear much fruit" (v. 5).
- "As the Father has loved me, so I have loved you; abide in my love" (v. 9).
- "If you keep my commandments, you will abide in my love" (v. 10).
- "This is my commandment, that you love one another as I have loved you" (v. 12).

What an amazing progression of thought! We are called upon by Jesus to abide or to dwell in Him. This abiding in Jesus means to abide in His love. In order to abide in His love, we must keep His commandments. And just when we're about to scurry off again to figure out just how long that list of commandments is, and what commandments are on that list, Jesus adds the final touch—the touch, we might say, of His finger writing in the earth of God's creation. "This is my commandment, that you love one another as I have loved you" (v. 12). To believe in Jesus as God's Son, the Word become flesh, is to live in obedience to that one single command. Believing in Jesus means being directed by Jesus to love one another—which means to love one another in the local church congregation, where we meet for worship, fellowship, and instruction with fellow disciples of Jesus. That is the one word, the one commandment, the single message flowing from the very heart and character of God *from the beginning*.

The Pharisees who dragged the humiliated and terrified woman into the presence of Jesus that day had turned a deaf ear to the Word that was in the beginning and from the beginning. They shouted out their verses of condemnation and capital punishment, backing it all up with the authority of Moses the prophet of God. They had their Bible on their side. They had scriptural support.

In reply, "Jesus bent down and wrote with his finger on the ground."

John 9:6

HE SPAT ON THE GROUND AND MADE
MUD WITH THE SALIVA AND SPREAD
THE MUD ON THE MAN'S EYES.

How to Recognize the Antichrist

Now here's a topic that grabs people's attention! How many books and pamphlets have been written; how many sermons preached and detailed charts drawn; how many accusations voiced and speculations offered regarding this issue of the Antichrist? Now add to the list: How many movies have been made that deal with the Antichrist and all the havoc he will wreak in the end times?

In the last half-century alone there have been many candidates for this dubious honor of Antichrist. Protestants used to assume it was the pope, while at least a few Catholics undoubtedly suspected Luther. Adolf Hitler would appear to have been a more likely nominee than either of them. In the past few decades alone, after Hitler, the leading candidates have included Henry Kissinger, Menachem Begin, and

Saddam Hussein—though to be sure Hussein's stock has fallen sharply in recent times. Every now and then in the grocery store checkout stands we find the latest scoop on the Antichrist from the likes of the *National Enquirer* and *Star* magazine. Occasionally a headline will run in one of those eminently reputable news sources about JFK—that despite the appearances and what history books might claim, Kennedy is being secretly kept on life-support so that one day he can emerge as the Antichrist figure, replete with head wounds that appeared to have killed him but apparently did not (cf. Rev. 13:3). There have been loads of elaborate and imaginative speculation about the identity of the Antichrist, most of which—if not all of which—belong in the "round file" situated on the floor next to your desk.

The fact is, the actual term *antichrist* is not found at all where we likely would expect it, the Book of Revelation. Instead, it appears only in the Epistles of John (1 John 2:18-22; 4:1-3; 2 John 7). We read first of all that "the liar" is "the one who denies that Jesus is the Christ . . . This is the antichrist, the one who denies the Father and the Son" (1 John 2:22). Later in 1 John we are counseled not to believe "every spirit, but [to] test the spirits to see whether they are from God; for many false prophets have gone out into the world" (4:1). We are then offered the criterion for making judgments regarding which prophetic utterances or "spirits" we should believe: "Every spirit that confesses that Jesus Christ has come in the flesh is from God, and every spirit that does not confess Jesus is not from God." John then warns that this spirit of denying Jesus (specifically, Jesus as "Christ" *and* Jesus as "flesh") is "the spirit of the antichrist, of which you have heard that it is coming; and now it is already in the world" (vv. 2-3). We find the same idea in John's brief second letter: "Many deceivers have gone out into the world, those who do not confess that Jesus Christ has come in the flesh; any such person is the deceiver and the antichrist!" (2 John 7).

We need to ask ourselves, What is going on here? What is the nature of the denial that John is so adamantly warning against?

We first read that the basic lie of the Antichrist is the denial that Jesus is the Christ. We recall that on one occasion Jesus asked His disciples who people were saying that He was, and after a litany of replies Jesus asked a more pressing question: "But who do you say that I am?" (Matt. 16:15). Peter was bold to reply, "You are the Messiah, the Son of the living God" (v. 16). Jesus was enthusiastic in His response to Peter, calling him "blessed" or "happy" for providing the right answer, but also carefully giving credit to "my Father in heaven" for having revealed this messianic identity to Peter (v. 17). But if we quickly read further, we find that *from that time on* Jesus began to tell His disciples about what awaited Him in Jerusalem: "great suffering," death, and resurrection (v. 21). It is crucial to the gospel message that Peter, who had offered his divinely revealed confession that Jesus is the Christ, was also the disciple who protested most vigorously that suffering and miserable death "must never happen" to Jesus. After all, He is the Christ, the Messiah, the Son of the living God! And so the same Jesus who had only recently congratulated Peter was now forced to rebuke Peter and to reject his protests regarding the great suffering to which Jesus was heading. And herein lies the rub.

Peter wanted very much to believe that Jesus was the Messiah, God's Anointed One, who would be Israel's deliverer. But Peter's idea of God's Messiah did not include the possibility of suffering and death. He did not expect—and likely would not want—such a bent-down Christ as that! He did not question that Jesus was "flesh," that Jesus was a real live human being like himself; that would not have been the issue for Peter. But he did question the possibility that Jesus could, or would, suffer greatly—surely not, if indeed He was the Messiah! Peter would not have questioned Jesus' capacity to suffer and die; but he *would* have likely assumed that if Jesus did suffer terribly and then die, that Jesus could not be the Messiah. That's not what Messiahs do. Presumably this is why the pair of disheartened disciples on the road to Emmaus, after Jesus' crucifixion, could say, "But we had hoped that he was the one to redeem Israel" (Luke 24:21).

Within a couple of generations after the time of Jesus' earthly ministry, however, a different but related issue began to arise. A growing number of people did believe that Jesus was indeed the Christ—but precisely because they believed that, they harbored doubts that Jesus really was human. For them the title "Christ" tended to mean a heavenly deliverer, an emissary from the spiritual realm (or God) sent down to deliver His followers from the material world, with its evils and hardships, and take them to heaven. They tended to think in very strong dualisms about spirit (identified with goodness) and matter (identified with evil). If Jesus was the Christ, the emissary of the heavenly realm—as in fact they believed—then Jesus could not really also be "flesh." Such a truly spiritual being could not also be part, parcel, and participant in the material world of physical bodies. We might put it this way: while the issue for Peter was whether this human being Jesus was really *the Christ,* for this growing number of so-called Christians at the turn of the first century, the issue was whether *the Christ* could really have been a human being at all. It is the "spirit" of these superspiritual people that the writings of John identify as antichrist.

In Christian thought such people are typically identified as Docetists, which comes from the Greek word *dokeō*—"to seem" or "to appear." The Docetists were happy to believe that a figure called Jesus was the Christ, indeed that this Jesus was the Son of God. In fact, it was precisely because they believed these things about Him that they felt they must deny that He had truly come "in the flesh." He only *appeared* to be a human being, because what is ultimately of the spiritual realm (i.e., God) cannot really and truly have entered into the realm of flesh—the realm of suffering, decay, struggle, aging, wrinkles, bleeding, and (sooner or later) death.

Please appreciate that these people were decidedly *spiritual.* Their Jesus Christ was never *really* flesh, blood, bone, and nerve endings. He was not given birth by a woman—ugh!—talk about a bloody, messy, painful process! One docetic teacher said that though it had appeared that the infant Jesus proceeded like a typical baby through the birth canal, He had in reality swooshed like "water through a tube" and landed—you almost get the picture of a feet-first landing—on the ground that He never really touched. In the middle of the second century, a teacher named Marcion gained widespread attention for his teaching that Jesus didn't even go through the appearances of childbirth; instead, He had simply appeared on planet Earth looking like a 30-year-old man. If they had known about holograms in the second century, that technology would have provided a ready analogy. Marcion denied that Jesus was ever a prenatal infant, ever given birth, ever circumcised (he naturally denied that Jesus was of Jewish lineage), ever dedicated in the Temple, or ever "increased in wisdom and in years, and in divine and human favor" (Luke 2:52). Like something out of *Star Trek,* according to Marcion Jesus sort of beamed down to our world looking like a human—but was not. If Jesus was a human being of flesh and blood, then how could He ever save us out of this evil material world?

Thus, it was all for "appearance's sake": Jesus never really got hungry, and He was only pretending (I suppose like a child who hates his peas) to eat; Jesus never really had to use the restroom (or the first-century Galilean equivalent), but just pretended to do so in order not to freak out His disciples; Jesus was never really tempted in all points as we are; Jesus didn't really die. Such events were all merely appearances. They had to be only that, for such distasteful and disgusting aspects of our humanity are all utterly beneath the dignity of deity. Christ the Son of God was too pure, too spiritual, to have been a real human being. There is nothing *bent-down* in the docetic story of Jesus.

In contrast, I think particularly of the story of Jesus bending down and spitting into the dirt to mold a mud salve for the blind man; of Jesus smearing the mudpacks on the man's eyes; of Jesus instructing the man to go and wash out his eyes in the Pool of Siloam (chapter 2 of this book). This is the *Christ* that we confess. The spirit of Antichrist recoils from this kind of incarnate (literally, "enfleshed") love.

These antichrists, then, were turning the gospel from the wonderful proclamation that the Word "became flesh and lived among us"—truly loved, truly bore our sorrows, truly touched the leper, truly embraced the sinner, truly bled and died on a Roman crucifix for our sins, truly was raised by God from the dead—into a decidedly *spiritual* religiosity.

This, according to the writings of John, is the very spirit of the Antichrist. It is the denial that the specific, first-century Jewish man of Nazareth, in Galilee, named Jesus—born, grew up, taught, suffered, died on a cross—*is the Christ, God's Anointed One.* Quite unlike popular speculations, the Antichrist is not some ugly monster or even some monstrous man but is instead a temptation—an ever-recurring temptation in the Church's history—to make Christianity too spiritual. While this may sound strange to our ears, this is how we recognize the spirit of the Antichrist. Remember the criterion John offers for discerning the Spirit of God: "Every spirit that confesses that Jesus Christ has come in the flesh is from God" (1 John 4:2). In other words, John was offering the Early Church (and us, too) a way to judge among the many spiritual voices that may make a variety of claims: whether it be the latest New Age fad or a vision someone has claimed to have received or the recent rage in some church circles over prophets and their revelations. In every case, John drives us back to the Word who became flesh. This is our revelation. It is particular, distinct, historical, and unrepeatable. When the Word became flesh and dwelt among us, that Incarnation occurred in, and as, Jesus of Nazareth. He is our criterion: a very specific, historical human being of flesh and nerve, of bone and blood.

There are some common ways in which the spirit
of the Antichrist can make its influence felt in the
Church, such as

- when we treat our own bodies as below the dignity of God's love and concern
- when we think that feeding the hungry or providing shelter for the homeless is not part of our Christian ministry
- when we think we can have a spiritual life that is somehow isolated and insulated from our everyday behaviors, our common activities and relationships, or
- when we live as though we assume that salvation is merely a matter of "going to heaven when I die," rather than of living a life of Christian obedience, here and now, as a bodily member of the Body of Christ in this world

The early second-century church leader Ignatius,
while on the road to Rome and his own martyrdom,
wrote a series of letters to churches along the way in
which he warned them, among other things, of this overly spiritual brand of Christianity that denied the truth
of the Incarnation. In one of his more passionate moments, he wrote to the Christians of Smyrna, "Pay close
attention to those who have wrong notions about the
grace of Jesus Christ, which has come to us, and note
how at variance they are with God's mind. They care
nothing about love: they have no concern for widows or
orphans, for the oppressed, for those in prison or released, for the hungry or the thirsty."[9]

Such people, we might add to Ignatius' warnings, are "at variance . . . with God's mind" because God's mind has been revealed, made clear, *taken on human existence* in the real human being Jesus Christ. Because of the Incarnation, we know that God's mind is invested in the goodness and redemption of the material creation; we know that God is not so spiritual as not also to be earthy; we know that God is love; and we know that God's love is a tender, compassionate embrace for the vulnerable ones, the oppressed ones, the imprisoned, the hungry and thirsty. Those who deny that the human being Jesus of Nazareth is God's Christ —or to say it another way, those who deny that the Christ could and would enter in so deeply in material creation so as to actually share in its risks and aches and joys—would have no reason why they should care about such matter(s).

Ignatius judged such people to be too "religious," too "spiritual"—or in the old saying, "too heavenly minded to be of any earthly good."

True Christian teaching, on the other hand, leads us to confess that heaven has come to earth—in Jesus Christ. Because of the Incarnation of the Word, to be truly heavenly-minded as Christians will unavoidably lead us to being of practical, everyday, down-to-earthly good.

When will we live like this? When will we love like this?

John 13:14

SO IF I, YOUR LORD AND TEACHER,
HAVE WASHED YOUR FEET,
YOU ALSO OUGHT TO WASH
ONE ANOTHER'S FEET.

Bent-Down Love in the Church

We have already seen in chapter 3 that John's Gospel offers a most amazing perspective on the authority and power of God. John tells us that during that final Passover meal, "Jesus, *knowing that the Father had given all things into his hands*, and that he had come from God and was going to God, got up from the table, took off his outer robe, . . . and began to wash his disciples' feet" (13:3-5). With all that power in His hands, Jesus' hands embraced the grimy feet of His friends in this lowly and humble task. The power of God is the power to serve. No other idea could really make sense of the Johannine proclamation that "God is love" (1 John 4:8, 16).

It was the very next day that those same hands—the hands into which God the Father had given all things—were nailed to a Roman cross. The Cross was indeed a sign of power too. It was a sign of Roman power, a constant and grim reminder of who was in power, who had control of the land of Judea and beyond. Thousands of Jewish men were crucified during the years of Roman rule, always for the purpose of reminding the underling people that they had no power to resist or to rebel against the authority of Rome. This is the power of violence, of weapons, of irresistible force. It is no stretch to say that this is the power of "shock and awe."

But it is not the power of God.

Jesus, knowing that He had come from God and was returning to God, got on His knees and washed feet. Jesus, knowing that He was God's very Word become flesh and living among us, offered over His hands and body to the violent, bloody power of human political authority. The power of God is the power to love. It is the power to lay down one's life for others.

We find, not surprisingly, that the letter of 1 John applies this fundamental Christian truth to the life of the Church, the fellowship of Jesus' disciples. We recall that this is the letter that teaches us to confess that "God is love"—and this would be a beautiful but vague sentiment if we did not find in this same letter a good working definition of what "love" is. But we do, for in 1 John 3:16 we read, "We know love by this, that he laid down his life for us." If we believe that whoever has seen Jesus has seen the Father because Jesus through His deeds and words has made God known, then we must also believe that Jesus' laying down of His life on the Cross is the ultimate act of revealing God. We know love by this; we know God by this. It was this marvelous truth that moved Charles Wesley to pen these lyrics:

Amazing love, how can it be?
that Thou my God wouldst die for me!

When we sing a song like that, it is not difficult to become caught up in the great joy and reverie of such love. Jesus died for me! But two considerations immediately arise. *First,* John writes that Jesus "laid down his life for *us,*" which means it's not "all about me" but about the "us" of the Church, the fellowship of Christian believers that Jesus has created by His death for us. This should move us immediately to a deep consideration for those fellow folk in the pews with whom we sing about God's "amazing love." *Second,* that is exactly where John takes us! "We know love by this," he writes, "that he laid down his life for us—*and* we ought to lay down our lives for one another" (1 John 3:16).

This is not at all unlike what Jesus said to His disciples. "If I, your Lord and Teacher, have washed your feet, you also ought to wash one another's feet" (John 13:14). But if in John's Gospel we are enjoined to live with one another in a way that is consistent with Jesus' act of washing feet, in John's first letter we are gathered at the foot of Jesus' cross. *Love one another like this,* John writes.

We have considered this before, but it is worth re-

peating: In both of these texts (and in fact highly char-
acteristic of the Johannine writings) the emphasis is on
"one another." Wash one another's feet. Lay down your
lives for one another. In the fellowship of Jesus' disciples we are called to a life of mutual servanthood, mutual loving and giving. If we live this way with one another, then no one is only a servant, only giving and
giving and never receiving. We are called to love and
also to receive love, to serve and also to be served, to
lay down our lives and also to receive the lives that our
brothers and sisters in Christ lay down for us.

This is not left in the realm of the theoretical or
the ideal. It is deeply practical. When Jesus washed
feet, He really held those smelly, funny-looking toes
and gently caressed them with real water and the flesh
of His hands. When Jesus laid down His life for us,
those same hands really were nailed to wood and bled
real blood. Similarly, when John writes that we likewise
ought to lay down our lives for one another, he does
not leave it as a flowery sentiment. He immediately
asks a probing and provocative question: "How does
God's love abide in anyone who has the world's goods
and sees a brother or sister in need and yet refuses
help?" (3:17).

Let us get as practical about this as John's letter
does. This means, at the simplest level, that no Christian
believer should ever languish for lack of food, shelter,
clothing, or medical help. If we really believe that Jesus
laid down His life for *us,* John is saying, then the *us* that

we are must really share that same sacrificial love with one another. Notice that so far we are not talking about what local congregations can or should do in addressing the needs of people outside the church. We are starting where John's Gospel, and John's letters, start: with one another in the fellowship of Jesus' disciples.

Clearly, however, this teaching extends us beyond our local congregations. Particularly in a world where communication and media technology make everyone on the planet virtually our next-door neighbor, we cannot help but see hundreds of thousands of Christian brothers and sisters in need. It is also no secret where the world's goods are largely to be found. They are in the hands of North Americans above all others. Christians of the United States and Canada have the world's goods like no other bodies of Christians on the planet.

We who live with far more than our share of the world's goods might be tempted to reply, "Well, thank God for the blessings we enjoy. We must be doing something right. So let us bless God for the goods we are given and pray that God will bless those other poor folk too—if they deserve it." In other words, we often tend all too easily to assume that "the Father has given all [these] things into [our] hands" (John 13:3). But even if indeed that is so—and if we take seriously what Jesus says to us as His disciples—we know that what God has given us is to be poured out in servanthood and love. We cannot ignore what Jesus did with the power, privilege, and authority that were entrusted into

His hands. He did not clench His hands into fists of strong-armed authority or possessiveness; instead, He opened His hands and gently washed feet—and in doing so created a new kind of fellowship. Further, the fellowship of mutual love, of giving and receiving, that Jesus has brought into being crosses all political borders, all ethnicities and languages, all social barriers. In this international, boundary-breaking fellowship called the Church we are to love one another "not in word or speech, but in truth and action" (1 John 3:18).[10]

This might leave one issue lingering. Is it only with fellow believers that Christians are called upon to share the world's goods? Do we draw the line at the church's walls? While we intuitively know that this is not the case, at the same time I want to underscore the great emphasis that John's Gospel and letters place upon the "one another" of Christian discipleship. It is undoubtedly not only the Christian in need that we are called upon to help but certainly *first* the Christian in need that we are called upon to help. In this way we underscore the fact that this truly is a fellowship, a community of Jesus' disciples, that we are a part of. It is noteworthy that Jesus said to those of freshly cleaned feet, "Just as I have loved you, you also should love one another. By this everyone will know that you are my disciples, if you have love for one another" (John 13:34-35). Jesus does not say that people outside the fellowship of disciples ("everyone") will know Jesus' disciples by how those disciples love them, but by how those disciples love each other. The testimony, in other words, is a communal and corporate testimony that every local congregation is to offer. As a second-century observer said of the Early Church, "Behold how they love one another!" Indeed, in His high priestly prayer Jesus prayed that His disciples would live in love and unity "so that the world may believe that you have sent me" (John 17:21).

Again, this need not at all imply that Christian compassion for the needy be limited to needy Christians. But it does imply that the Church, as a world-wide fellowship of Christian discipleship, is to be a community in which compassionate sharing is the rule of life with one another. People outside that community will be drawn to it precisely because of how we love one another. Such a corporate life of mutual love and service provides a powerful communal testimony to the rest of the world about how God intends that human beings should live with one another. In this way, when the Church does extend its goods and services to those beyond its walls, it does so precisely *as the Church,* a community of Christian compassion. In this way the love of Jesus' disciples for one another spills out and over into the world. But if there is no mutual love flowing within and throughout that community of Christian discipleship, then there is really nothing that can flow outward to those outside—and then there is also nothing on the inside that would be worth inviting the people on the outside to enter.

I suppose that is why Jesus instructed His disciples to wash one another's feet, rather than to go out and wash the feet of everyone they meet. Start at home, create a spiritual home of foot washing people, and many of those on the outside, dirty feet and all, will come looking for a home like that.

1 John 1:3

WE DECLARE TO YOU WHAT WE HAVE
SEEN AND HEARD SO THAT YOU
ALSO MAY HAVE FELLOWSHIP
WITH US; AND TRULY OUR
FELLOWSHIP IS WITH THE
FATHER AND WITH HIS
SON JESUS CHRIST.

The Bent-Down Life of Fellowship

"We declare to you what we have seen and heard," we read in the letter of 1 John as part of its introduction. But what is it that the apostles had "seen and heard"? This is no reference to generalities. Rather, "We declare to you what was from the beginning, what we have *heard,* what we have *seen* with our eyes, what we have looked at and touched with our hands, *concerning the Word of life*" (v. 1). They had seen and heard, they had touched—and been touched by—Jesus Christ, God's Living Word become living human being among us.

But, we might well object, that was 2,000 years ago! "If only I could see Jesus now," we might say. "Those apostles had an unfair advantage. They could hear Jesus teach and watch Him heal people. They could reach out and touch Him.

We're so far away from that time when He walked the earth."

Sometimes people even use this line of reasoning to reject Christianity, or a belief in God at all. "When God appears to me, then I'll believe," some say. "Why should I believe in something I can't see with my own eyes or touch with my own hands or hear with my own ears?"

Such questions should not be disrespected. We who are Christians do confess a demanding faith, for we believe that God has spoken the final and decisive Divine Word in Jesus Christ the Son (John 1:14; Heb. 1:1-2). This Word isn't the kind of word that everybody can just hear any old time; this Word was a human being who lived in a particular part of the world during a specific period of time. Theologians call this "the scandal of particularity," that God's Son dwelt among us under specific and particular historical conditions. The scandal of particularity affirms just the one Incarnation of the Son of God—in the person of Jesus of Nazareth, in Galilee, about two millennia in our planet's past.

So is it perhaps just a bit of "cold comfort" to know that there *were* people—people who themselves are now long gone—who heard, who saw with their eyes, who touched the very skin of the Word become flesh? How does that help us now, and here, in our time and place?

Of course we can reply that the Holy Spirit is the presence of God—the Spirit of the living Christ who

lives within our hearts, and who lives within the fellowship of the Church. This is, in fact, a very important as-
pect of Christian faith and experience. But talk about
the Spirit can quickly move us away from the precise
emphasis we have encountered repeatedly in the writings of John: the bent-down, earthy, tangible nature of
God Incarnate in Jesus. That is already a strong tendency among Christians—to overspiritualize the faith, to
remove the bodily realities of hearing, seeing, and
touching with which 1 John begins. For that matter, we
have already seen in chapter 7 that we can know and
recognize the activity of the Spirit of God as the Spirit
who "confesses that Jesus Christ has come in the flesh"
(1 John 4:2); thus, for us the work of the Spirit is always faithfully leading us back to the Jesus of history,
the One who "has come in the flesh." Somehow, hearing, seeing, and touching must continue to be pro-
foundly important to our Christian faith and life.

In this light, I believe there is a basic point in this
opening of 1 John that we often overlook. In verse 2 we
read that "the eternal life that was with the Father and
was revealed to us"—which can only refer to the Word
of Life, the Word that was with God and was God and
became flesh among us—"we declare to you." But *why*?
Why does John say that he and his fellow apostles proclaim the Word who became flesh? The answer to that
simple question is significant and profound: They do
so, he writes, "so that you also may have fellowship
with us" (1 John 1:3).

The point is, John doesn't begin by saying, "We declare to you what was from the beginning, what we heard and saw and touched with our own hands, the very Word of life, so that you can believe that He once walked the earth"! He doesn't even say, "We declare all this to you so that the Holy Spirit can enter into your heart." He says, "We declare [all this] . . . so that you also may have *fellowship* with us."

This term *fellowship* is the term most often used to translate the Greek word *koinonia,* and it really is a workable translation. *Koinonia* means a sharing together in something, or mutual participation. When we translate it with the word *fellowship,* we are talking about life that is shared together with one another. That, according to John, is what the life of the Church is supposed to be like.

The obvious implication is that this life of fellowship is "the eternal life that was with the Father and was revealed to us" in Christ, "the Word of life." The *life* of which Jesus Christ is the *Word* is the life of fellowship, the life of sharing together. The further, less obvious, but inescapable implication is that this kind of life flows from the very heart of who God is. The "eternal life" that John is talking about here is not primarily living forever. It is not first of all a quantity of life; rather, it is the divine quality of life, the kind of life that God is—and the kind of life that God shares. If God is love, then God is life that shares. God is self-giving, other-receiving love.

This is why John continues, "and truly our fellowship is with the Father and with his Son Jesus Christ" (1 John 1:3). The life of sharing into which we are invited by the gospel is the very life shared by the Father and the Son. It is the life of fellowship, and we human beings, too, can share in this life through the outpouring of the gift of the Holy Spirit. The Spirit is the shared life of God, flowing through Jesus the Son into our very lives. John's Gospel dramatizes this marvelous truth by describing the resurrected Jesus in the midst of His frightened and confused disciples: "'Peace be with you. As the Father has sent me, so I send you.' When he had said this, he breathed on them and said to them, 'Receive the Holy Spirit'" (John 20:21-22). To receive the Holy Spirit is to receive the very outpoured life of fellowship, of mutual sharing together, that is none other than God.

It is this generous, wondrous gift of the Spirit that can make it possible for a church to exist as an answer —we may hope and trust—to Jesus' own high priestly prayer:

- "I ask . . . that they may all be one" (John 17:20-21a).
- "As you, Father, are in me and I am in you, may they also be in us" (v. 21b).
- "The glory that you have given me, I have given them, so that they may be one, as we are one" (v. 22).
- "I in them and you in me, that they may become

completely one, so that the world may know that you have sent me" (v. 23).

Amazing!

Jesus prays that His circle of disciples—not only the immediate circle but all those who would come to believe through their gospel proclamation (17:20)— would actually, here and now, and in this life, live together in the life of fellowship. Only the actual and active presence of the Spirit could bring this kind of life into local Christian congregations. And how often do we fall far short of this kind of life, this *eternal life* (v. 2; 1 John 1:1-4)! What Jesus is praying for, essentially, is a sanctified Church! This is a fellowship of Christian disciples who love one another as Christ has loved us, who wash one another's feet, who day after day live this mutually shared life together in the power of the Spirit.

I have wondered lately if Jesus really meant it when He prayed that. If He did—and I really think He did—then the 2,000 years or so since that prayer was first prayed must have been deeply and painfully frustrating. For that circle of disciples that has become the Church worldwide over the past millennia has not exactly provided a living model of fellowship. Instead we have argued and fought; often we have ignored, other times even killed, each other—all too often in the name of Jesus. We have splintered into virtually numberless denominations, but even within denominations the backbiting, the competition, the one-upmanship continue. And the local church?

My Sunday School teacher Reuben Welch has even jolted his class by asking us if we think Jesus is still praying this very prayer. After all, it hasn't really been answered yet! If in fact Jesus intercedes for us (Rom. 8:34), if He "always lives to make intercession" (Heb. 7:25) for us, then it surely makes sense that His intercessions include the kinds of requests He made, in behalf of His followers, back in John 17. If that is true, Jesus is truly a patient and longsuffering High Priest— a bent-down intercessor—in our behalf. His prayer has not been answered.

I believe we should take Jesus' praying for us very seriously. We certainly should not shrug it off and assume that it can only happen in heaven or in the age to come. After all, Jesus prayed this for His disciples, His Church, so that the world might believe that the Father has sent the Son (17:21). The great evangelistic tool of Jesus' high priestly prayer is a sanctified Church, where divine life and love are so freely shared that the world can see the difference. If that is true, then it cannot be shoved off as impossible in this life, achievable only in some heavenly realm.

In fact, the very point is, as we have seen already, that the heavenly realm has already come to us. "This life was revealed, and we have seen it and testify to it, and declare to you the eternal life that was with the Father and was revealed to us" in none other than Jesus Christ (1 John 1:2). And let us not forget that this eternal life, this heavenly realm, has been declared in order that all who believe might share together in this wonderful, divine life *here and now*—"so that you also may have fellowship with us" (v. 3).

So we return to the original problem of this final chapter. What about the fact that Jesus lived so long ago, so far away? What about the fact that we cannot see Him with our eyes, cannot hear His words with our ears, cannot touch Him with our hands?

It comes down to this: What faces, what bodies *can* you see? Whose voice, whose words, whose cries *can* you hear? Whose skin *can* you touch with your own hands? Who *can* you feed and clothe and shelter? It is this letter of 1 John, after all, that reminds us that "those who do not love a brother or sister whom they have seen, cannot love God whom they have not seen" (4:20). No one has ever seen God; further, we are among the vast majority of Christians who have never seen Jesus' face or felt the touch of His hand—*however,* John insists, "If we love one another, God lives in us, and his love is perfected in us" (v. 12).

I think of three different Resurrection encounters, all recorded uniquely in John's Gospel. First are Jesus' words to Mary, the very first witness to the Resurrection, in the tomb garden: "Do not hold on to me, because I have not yet ascended to the Father" (20:17). Sometimes I have thought it would have made more sense for Jesus to say, "Hold on to Me while you can, because I'm about to ascend to the Father." But instead Jesus instructs Mary not to try to grasp Him, not to hold on to Him as if to reassure herself that Jesus' physical presence, having now returned, would never leave again. I have, then, come to suspect that the logic of Jesus' statement is more along these lines: "Do not hold on to Me, because I don't want you getting used to it—I am about to ascend to the Father." Do not try to hang on to this moment, this encounter, miraculous and wonderful as it is. Jesus' words discourage Mary from latching on to Him as a body that can be touched—for very soon He would not be.

Next, I think of Jesus' second appearance among His disciples in a locked-down room, this time with Thomas present (20:26ff.). Here Jesus says to Thomas, who has voiced his doubts regarding the reality of his friends' experience the week before, "Put your finger here and see my hands. Reach out your hand and put it in my side. Do not doubt but believe" (v. 27). It surely is significant that Jesus' resurrection did not remove His wounds; He bore the scars in His hands and side, and there is absolutely no reason to think that He does not still. His resurrected body will bear the marks of divine love—the love of Jesus laying down His life for us—into all eternity. The Resurrection did not, does not, and shall not undo His bent-down character. The Father put all things into His hands—and for all ages those hands will be nail-scarred hands that are noticeably adept at breaking bread and washing feet.

For all of that, it is also significant that there is no evidence that Thomas actually did try to touch Jesus. Perhaps he did, but the Gospel makes no point of telling us so. It implies, in fact, that just seeing Jesus was enough. Hence the Resurrected One says, "Have you believed because you have seen me? Blessed are those who have not seen and yet have come to believe" (v. 28). Just as Jesus was weaning Mary away from the idea that He would be a constant physical presence to touch, so now He was weaning Thomas and the other disciples away from the expectation that He would be readily visible much longer.

Finally, I think of that encounter of the resurrected Jesus with Peter and a few other disciples by the Sea of Galilee (John 21; see chapter 4). We have marveled at this radically unexpected posture in which we find the resurrected Lord, the very Son of God, into whose hands all things have been given. He is bent down by the charcoal fire, cooking fish and warming bread. It's a mind-blower: Jesus poking at the fire with a stick, keeping the coals alive, and saying, "Come and have breakfast" (21:12).

But the same point can, and must, be made that was made with Mary and with Thomas. Jesus probably won't be cooking your breakfast for you tomorrow morning. This One who was seen and heard and felt by human hands is no longer present with us in that way. He won't be starting the fire in your fireplace this evening when it gets cold. But He does ask you, as He asked Peter, "Do you love me?" Perhaps He adds, "Do you love Me, though you do not see Me with your eyes? Can you love Me though you do not touch Me with your hands?"

And if we reply as Peter did, then we know what Jesus is expecting of us: *Feed My sheep.*

As we feed and are fed by others, we extend the fellowship of Jesus' lakeside breakfast that early misty morn. When "Jesus came and took the bread and gave it to them, and did the same with the fish" (v. 13), He was inviting them into the reality of fellowship, into "the eternal life that was with the Father and was revealed" (1 John 1:2) to them by Jesus' bent-down presence. Now it is our turn to feed His disciples, His friends, His sheep—and also to be fed.

Come and dine, the Master calleth. Come and dine, and feed Jesus' sheep even as you are fed. Then no one of Jesus' friends will go hungry, none will get cold. Then, too, the world will know—by the power of the Spirit of the life of fellowship—that the Father has sent the Son.

May it be so, and in our days.

NOTES

1. Kosuke Koyama, *No Handle on the Cross: An Asian Meditation on the Crucified Mind* (Maryknoll, New York: Orbis Books, 1977).

2. *Library of Christian Classics*, Vol. I, ed. Cyril C. Richardson (Philadelphia: Westminster Press, 1953), 110.

3. Koyama, *No Handle on the Cross*, 11.

4. Ibid., 12.

5. Ibid.

6. Charles Wesley, *Hymns of Petition and Thanksgiving for the Promise of the Father*, No. 28 (1746).

7. Gayle D. Erwin, *The Jesus Style* (Palm Springs, Calif.: Ronald N. Haynes Publishers, Inc., 1983), 147.

8. Ibid.

9. *Library of Christian Classics*, Vol. I, 114.

10. For ways in which one can become involved in sharing our resources with brothers and sisters who have much less, check online at Nazarene Compassionate Ministries: www.ncm.org.

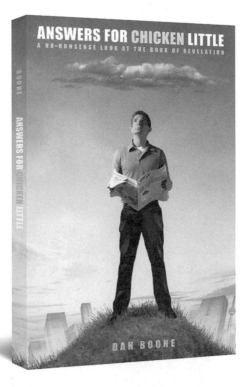

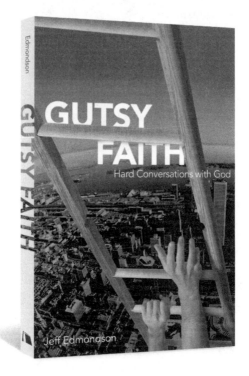